Modern Middle East Nations
AND THEIR STRATEGIC PLACE IN THE WORLD

DJIBOUTI

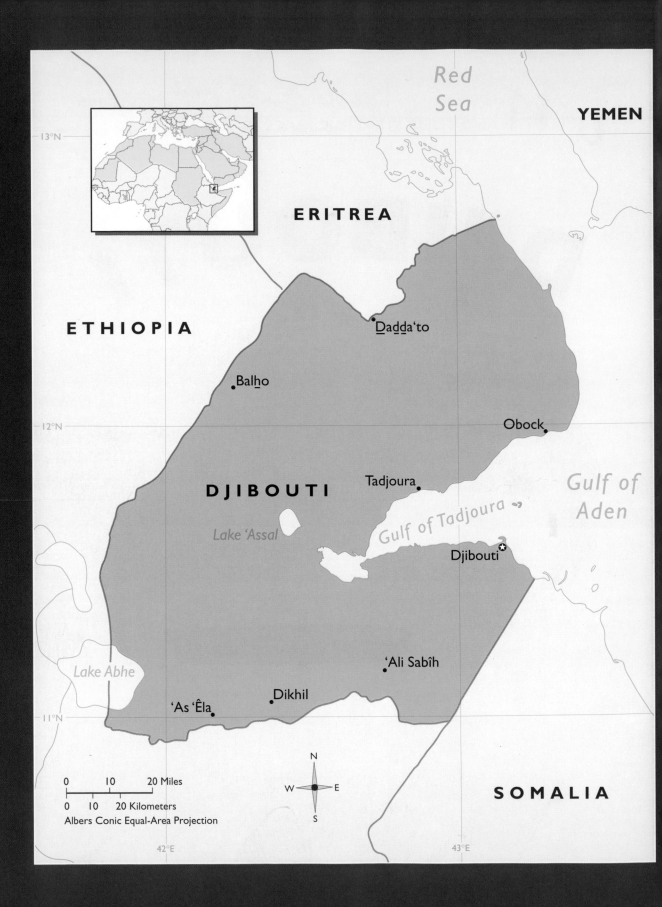

Modern Middle East Nations
AND THEIR STRATEGIC PLACE IN THE WORLD

DJIBOUTI

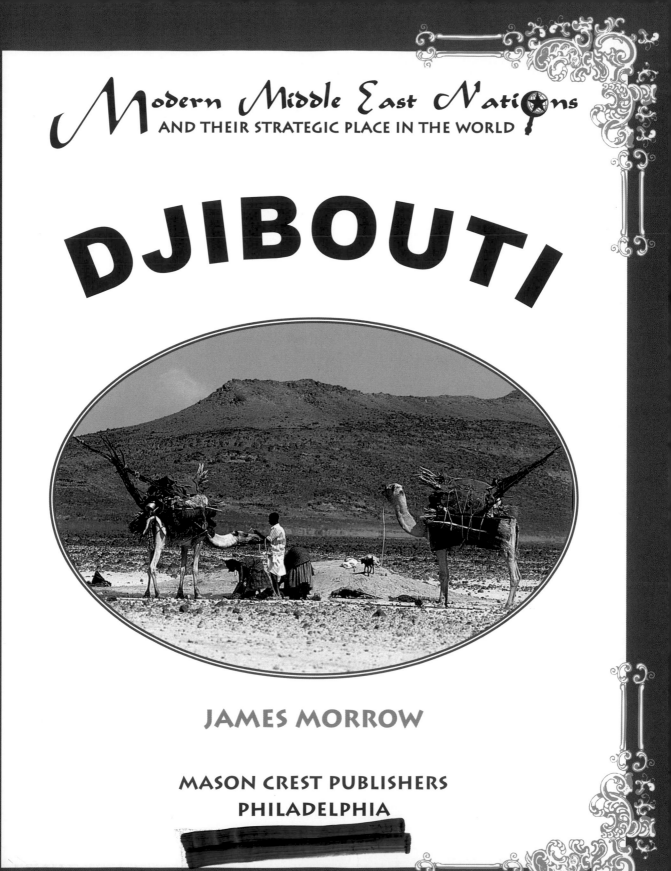

JAMES MORROW

MASON CREST PUBLISHERS
PHILADELPHIA

Produced by OTTN Publishing, Stockton, New Jersey

Mason Crest Publishers
370 Reed Road
Broomall, PA 19008
www.masoncrest.com

First printing

1 3 5 7 9 8 6 4 2

Library of Congress Cataloging-in-Publication Data

Morrow, James, 1974–
  Djibouti / James Morrow.
    p. cm. — (Modern Middle East nations and their strategic
place in the world)
Summary: Discusses the geography, history, economy, government,
religion, people, foreign relations, and communities of Djibouti.
Includes bibliographical references and index.
  ISBN 1-59084-525-0
1. Djibouti—Juvenile literature. [1. Djibouti.] I. Title. II. Series.
DT411.22.M67 2003
967.71—dc21

                                                                2003000900

TABLE OF CONTENTS

Modern Middle East Nations
AND THEIR STRATEGIC PLACE IN THE WORLD

Dr. Harvey Sicherman, president and director of the Foreign Policy Research Institute, is the author of such books as *America the Vulnerable: Our Military Problems and How to Fix Them* (2002) and *Palestinian Autonomy, Self-Government and Peace* (1993).

Introduction

by Dr. Harvey Sicherman

Situated as it is between Africa, Europe, and the Far East, the Middle East has played a unique role in world history. Often described as the birthplace of religions (notably Judaism, Christianity, and Islam) and the cradle of civilizations (Egypt, Mesopotamia, Persia), this region and its peoples have given humanity some of its most precious possessions. At the same time, the Middle East has had more than its share of conflicts. The area is strewn with the ruins of fortifications and the cemeteries of combatants, not to speak of modern arsenals for war.

Today, more than ever, Americans are aware that events in the Middle East can affect our security and prosperity. The United States has a considerable military, political, and economic presence throughout much of the region. Developments there regularly find their way onto the front pages of our newspapers and the screens of our television sets.

Still, it is fair to say that most Middle Eastern countries remain a mystery, their cultures and religions barely known, their peoples and politics confusing and strange. The purpose of this book series is to change that, to educate the reader in the basic facts about the 23 states and many peoples that make up the region. (For our purpose, the Middle East also includes the North African states linked by ethnicity, language, and religion to the Arabs, as well as Somalia and Mauritania, which are African but share the Muslim religion and are members of the Arab League.) A notable feature of the series is the integration of geography, demography, and history; economics and politics; culture and religion. The careful student will learn much that he or she needs to know about ever so important lands.

A few general observations are in order as an introduction to the subject matter.

The first has to do with history and politics. The modern Middle East is full of ancient sites and peoples who trace their lineage and literature to antiquity. Many commentators also attribute the Middle East's political conflicts to grievances and rivalries from the distant past. While history is often invoked, the truth is that the modern Middle East political system dates only from the 1920s and was largely created by the British and the French, the victors of World War I. Such states as Algeria, Iraq, Israel, Jordan, Kuwait, Saudi Arabia, Syria, Turkey, and the United Arab Emirates did not exist before 1914—they became independent between 1920 and 1971. Others, such as Egypt and Iran, were dominated by outside powers until well after World War II. Before 1914, most of the region's states were either controlled by the Turkish-run Ottoman Empire or owed allegiance to the Ottoman sultan. (The sultan was also the caliph or highest religious authority in Islam, in the line of the prophet Muhammad's successors, according to the beliefs of the majority of Muslims known as the Sunni.) It was this imperial Muslim system that was ended by the largely British military victory over the Ottomans in World War I. Few of the leaders who emerged in the wake of this event were happy with the territories they were assigned or the borders, which were often drawn by Europeans. Yet, the system has endured despite many efforts to change it.

The second observation has to do with economics, demography, and natural resources. The Middle Eastern peoples live in a region of often dramatic geographical contrasts: vast parched deserts and high mountains, some with year-round snow; stone-hard volcanic rifts and lush semi-tropical valleys; extremely dry and extremely wet conditions, sometimes separated by only a few miles; large permanent rivers and wadis, riverbeds dry as a bone until winter rains send torrents of flood from the mountains to the sea. In ancient times, a very skilled agriculture made the Middle East the breadbasket of the Roman Empire, and its trade carried luxury fabrics, foods, and spices both East and West.

Most recently, however, the Middle East has become more known for a single commodity—oil, which is unevenly distributed and largely concentrated in the Persian Gulf and Arabian Peninsula (although large pockets are also to be found in Algeria, Libya, and other sites). There are also new, potentially lucrative offshore gas fields in the Eastern Mediterranean.

This uneven distribution of wealth has been compounded by demographics. Birth rates are very high, but the countries with the most oil are often lightly populated. Over the last decade, Middle East populations under the age of 20 have grown enormously. How will these young people be educated? Where will they work? The failure of most governments in the region to give their people skills and jobs (with notable exceptions such as Israel) has also contributed to large out-migrations. Many have gone to Europe; many others work in other Middle Eastern countries, supporting their families from afar.

Another unsettling situation is the heavy pressure both people and industry have put on vital resources. Chronic water shortages plague the region. Air quality, public sanitation, and health services in the big cities are also seriously overburdened. There are solutions to these problems, but they require a cooperative approach that is sorely lacking.

A third important observation is the role of religion in the Middle East. Americans, who take separation of church and state for granted, should know that most countries in the region either proclaim their countries to be Muslim or allow a very large role for that religion in public life. Among those with predominantly Muslim populations, Turkey alone describes itself as secular and prohibits avowedly religious parties in the political system. Lebanon was a Christian-dominated state, and Israel continues to be a Jewish state. While both strongly emphasize secular politics, religion plays an enormous role in culture, daily life, and legislation. It is also important to recall that Islamic law (*Sharia*) permits people to practice Judaism and Christianity in Muslim states but only as *Dhimmi*, protected but very second-class citizens.

Fourth, the American student of the modern Middle East will be impressed by the varieties of one-man, centralized rule, very unlike the workings of Western democracies. There are monarchies, some with traditional methods of consultation for tribal elders and even ordinary citizens, in Saudi Arabia and many Gulf States; kings with limited but still important parliaments (such as in Jordan and

Morocco); and military and civilian dictatorships, some (such as Syria) even operating on the hereditary principle (Hafez al Assad's son Bashar succeeded him). Turkey is a practicing democracy, although a special role is given to the military that limits what any government can do. Israel operates the freest democracy, albeit constricted by emergency regulations (such as military censorship) due to the Arab-Israeli conflict.

In conclusion, the MODERN MIDDLE EAST NATIONS series will engage imagination and interest simply because it covers an area of such great importance to the United States. Americans may be relative latecomers to the affairs of this region, but our involvement there will endure. We at the Foreign Policy Research Institute hope that these books will kindle a lifelong interest in the fascinating and significant Middle East.

A mosque in Djibouti City, the capital of Djibouti. A great majority of Djiboutians are Muslims. Throughout the country's history they have had good trade relations with the Arabs of the Arabian Peninsula, located directly across the Bab el Mandeb Strait.

Place in the World

There is an old saying in Djibouti, a tiny country in a rocky and inhospitable corner of Africa: "Before crossing this country, even the jackal makes his will." Djibouti has a reputation—if largely undeserved—of being a difficult place to live. With its small population and size (it is slightly smaller than the state of Massachusetts), perhaps Djibouti has not yet been afforded a large enough audience to hear of its positive traits. For example, many people do not know that this country has a rich geological history, and that it sits at one of the world's most important crossroads from trade.

The few Westerners who know Djibouti well generally speak of a place of continual interest and importance. Because of its strategic position on what is known as the **Horn of Africa**, practically a stone's throw across the Bab el Mandeb Strait from the Arabian Peninsula, Djibouti has been a keystone in political empires and commercial ventures for centuries. From the earliest days of ancient Egypt, whose people mythologized the land, through the different eras of the Greeks, Romans, and Muslim traders, Djibouti has been a major gateway to both the Red Sea and the Indian Ocean.

Long before the early traders crossed the Bab el Mandeb, the first of the human race may have roamed Djibouti's deserts. The present-day country lies adjacent to the famous **Great Rift Valley**, where many seminal scientific discoveries have been made. This valley cleaves Africa from Egypt to South Africa; within its reaches, paleontologists have found some of the earliest human fossils on record. "Lucy," the famous skull unearthed in 1974 that

Anthropologist Donald C. Johanson presents the ancient remains of "Lucy," a human ancestor his research team discovered in Hadar, Ethiopia, in 1974. Similar discoveries of human ancestors have been made in Ethiopia as well as neighboring countries like Djibouti, leading many scientists to believe that humankind originated in the Afar Triangle.

is believed to be the oldest known human remains, was dug up in Djibouti's northern neighbor, Ethiopia. The discovery's location is in the **Afar Triangle**, a region that includes Djibouti as well as Eritrea, a country directly north of Djibouti. Scientists have also made spectacular finds in Djibouti itself, and are hopeful that future digs in the country will reveal more about the origins of human life and civilization.

The key moments of Djibouti's history were not just during the prehistoric eras, however. In modern times, Djibouti had been an important yet often overlooked outpost of the French empire, which acquired the colony to keep the British from gaining strategic control of the region. Today, with France no longer a colonial force, Djibouti still plays a vital role in today's world affairs, hosting U.S. and German troops taking part in the "war on terrorism," which was begun in response to the September 2001 attacks on New York and Washington, D.C. Djibouti offers a safe base of operations that is close enough to often-hostile countries like Afghanistan and Iraq.

Djibouti and her neighbors also have a strategic position along the shipping lanes through which pass great quantities of oil. Not surprisingly, regional tensions are of great concern to the West. Conflicts between and within bordering countries like Eritrea, Ethiopia, and Somalia (located on the southeastern border) have often obstructed Western trade. For Djiboutians, the conflicts have been much more detrimental. One of the most significant conse-quences of regional conflict is the refugee crisis. As a result of var-ious wars in the Horn of Africa, at times as many as 200,000 refugees have lived in Djibouti. This presence of the refugees has helped contribute to the grinding poverty that is, unfortunately, a daily reality for almost every one of the over 470,000 who call Djibouti home.

Djibouti has long been an important port and staging area for empire maintenance and military campaigns, but it also has other

Pedestrians walk through a street intersection in Djibouti City, Djibouti. The seaport helps make this capital city a center for trade, though many say Djibouti's best natural and historical attractions lie elsewhere in the country.

facets that are often overlooked by historians, such as the history of its two main tribes, the **Afars** and **Issas**. Previously named French Somaliland, which was later changed to "the Territory of Afars and Issas," Djibouti is home to a rich cultural life, which is greatly the product of its central location. It is clear that the country has benefited by sitting at the crossroads of civilizations for many millennia.

Visitors who do not venture beyond the drab downtown of Djibouti City typically fail to see that Djibouti is a place of great beauty. It is home to a vast number of different birds, including several rare species, and a landscape that within a relatively tiny space contains a giant salt lake, a desolate lava field, and a game reserve. For those tourists adventurous enough to make the trip, Djibouti also is reported to offer some of the best scuba diving in the world.

Yet with all of this history, culture, and biodiversity packed into its tiny area, Djibouti has yet to appear on the radar screens of many scholars and travelers. Djibouti's hidden treasures may one day be completely revealed, but for the moment, it remains a place that a large segment of the world has not yet encountered.

Two camels greet each other in the desert. Camels are still a popular mode of transport in Djibouti, particularly in the volcanic desert region, which covers a large portion of the country's western half.

The Land

"It is truly a valley of hell here, hemmed in by stark mountains, and where everything seems tormented by an endless and hopeless struggle," wrote French traveler Henri de Monfried about Djibouti in 1937. He had several other complaints:

> Everywhere there are thorns: on the ground, on the bushes, on the trees; everything seems to want to scratch, to tear, to harm; souls in glassy hues of metallic oxide, rocks jutting out like monsters from the Apocalypse, trees with tortured boughs, it is all the stuff of nightmares and, in the distance, the howling of hyenas seems to personify the dismal voice of this harrowing nature.

When it comes to climate and landscape, Djibouti has never had a good reputation. Colonists from Europe who arrived in the region during the 19th and 20th centuries experienced an exceedingly dry climate, with an annual rainfall of only 5 inches (12.7 centimeters). They only saw

Djibouti as desolate and dangerous, and for the most part failed to see the charms that today's visitors have just now begun to discover. Its reputation for having a singularly fierce environment is somewhat misleading, for there is more beyond the somewhat seedy port city of Djibouti and the beaches that flank it. Djibouti actually boasts a surprising diversity of physical settings, environments, and wildlife, as well as a unique form of potential energy that could someday meet the country's power needs.

GEOLOGY

Although an obscure topic to most people, geology—the study of the earth's formation and its continual changes—is a fascinating discipline that in recent years has turned its sights on Djibouti. The country has become of great interest to geologists because it is situated at the meeting point of three of the world's ***tectonic plates***, which have shifted around the planet for millions of years, creating and destroying

The basin of Lake Assal, Djibouti's lowest point at 509 feet (155 meters) below sea level, was formed by a volcanic eruption. The country's subterranean activity, which causes volcanoes to erupt about every 50 years, is a potential source of geothermal energy.

A map showing Djibouti's major geographic features. The country's largest geographic zone is the volcanic desert in the west.

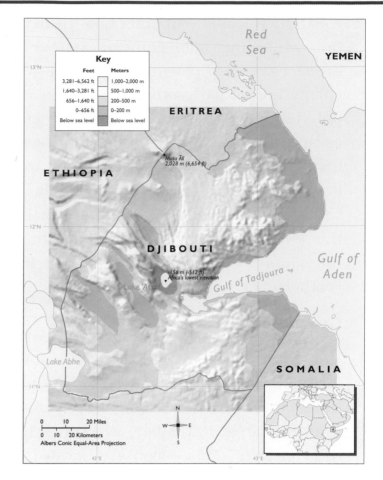

landmasses. Because Djibouti has such a unique orientation with the earth's plates, there is almost no other place on the planet where someone can witness geological history "in the making." The country's volcanoes, valleys, sunken plains, salt lakes, and great cleaving rifts are illustrations of the massive disruptions—past and present—under the surface of Djibouti. These movements are slowly but surely changing the country's—and the planet's—future. Scientists even speculate that in a few million years the plates will have caused Djibouti to split from Africa, and that it will float out to sea as part of a new continent.

Volcanoes erupt about every 50 years in Djibouti; the last major explosion took place in 1978 at Ardoukoba near Lake Assal. The constant volcanic eruptions take their toll on Djibouti's economy, but while the subterranean activity may scare off property investors, it also potentially provides a rare and efficient kind of energy known as "geothermal energy." This type of energy, which only Iceland and a few other countries use, takes the heat that escapes from the earth's crust to generate electricity and provide residential heating. While Djiboutians are not really in need of energy for heating, they could definitely use the electrical power. Unfortunately, like so many other worthwhile projects in Djibouti, the development of methods to tap into the energy is hampered by the country's lack of funds. Djibouti thus can scarcely hope for geothermal energy in the near future.

GEOGRAPHY

The 8,880 square miles (23,000 square kilometers) of Djibouti, including the 8 square miles (20 sq km) of water, are located in a the Afar Triangle, a triangular depression that is part of the dramatic Great Rift Valley, which nearly runs the entire length of the continent. This region was formed millions of year ago when volcanic activity under the sea pushed rock and lava up to the surface. As testimony that the country emerged from the sea, most of the lakes are saltwater instead of freshwater. Salt is abundant throughout the country, and for centuries it has provided Djiboutian merchants with a saleable commodity.

This is not to suggest, however, that Djibouti is nothing but salt and lava; the country is actually comprised of three separate and distinct geographical zones. The first zone is the coastal plains, which cover approximately 140 miles (225 km) of the country's coastline. Here, the land is distinguished by long stretches of mostly deserted sandy beaches, as well as soil that in certain places is good for agriculture. In the coastal plains, there are 9 square miles (24 square kilometers) of actual farmland, certainly not a sufficient portion to support several hundred thousand people.

Not surprisingly, many traces of Djibouti's ancient history can be found here, as inland tribes and traders from across the water set up towns—and eventually cities—in this one temperate region of the country. Hard as it may be to believe, considering the country's extreme heat, the weather is relatively cool in this region. The sea breezes moderate the high temperatures, which can reach 113°F (45°C) in the summertime.

In the north of the country lie the mountain ranges. Impressive peaks shoot out of the ground here; the highest mountain in the region is Moussa Ali, which reaches a height of over 6,600 feet (2,011 meters). The region also has some forests and patches of

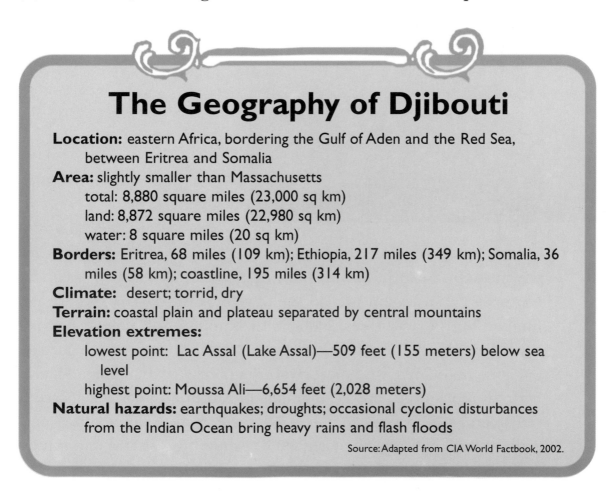

The Geography of Djibouti

Location: eastern Africa, bordering the Gulf of Aden and the Red Sea, between Eritrea and Somalia

Area: slightly smaller than Massachusetts
   total: 8,880 square miles (23,000 sq km)
   land: 8,872 square miles (22,980 sq km)
   water: 8 square miles (20 sq km)

Borders: Eritrea, 68 miles (109 km); Ethiopia, 217 miles (349 km); Somalia, 36 miles (58 km); coastline, 195 miles (314 km)

Climate: desert; torrid, dry

Terrain: coastal plain and plateau separated by central mountains

Elevation extremes:
   lowest point: Lac Assal (Lake Assal)—509 feet (155 meters) below sea level
   highest point: Moussa Ali—6,654 feet (2,028 meters)

Natural hazards: earthquakes; droughts; occasional cyclonic disturbances from the Indian Ocean bring heavy rains and flash floods

Source: Adapted from CIA World Factbook, 2002.

An Afar nomad poses in front of his camel. Over the centuries, the intensive grazing of camels and other pastoral animals has contributed to the depletion of Djibouti's grassland.

dense vegetation, but it has generally been a difficult place for anyone to live, except for the Afars who have called it their home for centuries. This region is also the site of Foret de Day, where fig, juniper, and acacia trees, along with bamboo and palms, provide cover for the wildlife. Among the species that live there are gazelle, baboons, monkeys, wild pigs, civet cats (skunk-like mammals), and hyrax (rabbit-sized, hoofed mammals). Although about 56 percent of Djibouti's land has some sort of tree growth, only about 1 percent of the country is considered proper forestland, and it is concentrated in these mountains.

The forests face Djibouti's most prevalent ecological crises—endangered wildlife and depleted grassland. Although the government formally outlawed hunting in 1971, the practice still goes on during Djibouti's frequent droughts. Hunters have done the most extensive damage in the areas where the majority of forest wildlife lives. Intensive grazing has also put pressure on the forests. It is estimated that the country is home to an astounding 1.5 million heads of cattle, sheep, goats, and camels, and that there are two animals for every Djiboutian citizen. Herders, especially goat and sheep owners, are evermore desperate to use suitable grazing land, and the forests greatly suffer for it.

To the west is the third and by far the largest of Djibouti's geographic zones—the volcanic desert. The region consists of arid, rocky wasteland, and is primarily what gives the country its reputation as a harsh, inhospitable place. The desert, which can support virtually no economic activity except for the production of salt, has been compared to the surface of the moon. The landscape here, especially along the salt lakes, is so otherworldly that much of the original science-fiction movie, *Planet of the Apes*, was filmed here. Real-life scientists, too, have thought to take advantage of the Djiboutian desert's lunar appearance; the European Space Agency, an organization much like the United States' NASA, once attempted to conduct tests on a lunar module in the desert. The tests, however, proved to be unsuccessful because the iron oxide and high salt content of the soil interfered with the equipment's radar.

Few foreigners have ventured across the land, but those who

Due to the slow but steady shifting of tectonic plates beneath the earth's surface, in a few million years Djibouti as we currently know it will no longer exist.

have usually return with a harrowing account. Sean Rorison, a visitor traveling by truck through the desert, offered this description:

> The landscape is stark yet beautiful—post-apocalyptic in many ways. There are gigantic dried-up lakes, revealing only fields of white salt deposits sitting on the desert floor. The road from Dikhil to Galafi goes into a valley for several hours, which is definitely below sea level. It was so hot in this valley that my fingertips would burn if I touched the window. . . . To navigate through this area without it would be impossible I think. The only creatures outside on the barren gravel and rock and salt were the occasional camel, and some odd-looking plant formations that must be sucking up the last of the water from the dried-up lakes.

WILDLIFE

Despite its harsh climate, Djibouti is also home to a surprising amount of wildlife. Djibouti's northern forests—while inhospitable to most humans—are home to a large number of African animals, although the variety of creatures and habitats hardly rivals those of Africa's more-famous safari destinations in Ethiopia, Kenya, and Tanzania. Much of Djibouti's wildlife consists of those species acclimated to desert and mountain climates; thus large populations of antelopes and oryx are found throughout the country. Monkeys and baboons are common, too, and are found in the forests and sometimes even in Djibouti town. Also common are a wide variety of reptiles, including deadly snakes, vipers, cobras, and mambas, as well as more-docile species such as tortoises. Hyenas and jackals are a familiar sight, though they are hated for the toll they take on domestic animal herds. Leopards are still seen occasionally, although they have been hunted nearly out of existence in Djibouti.

Djibouti has fascinating and diverse birdlife; some 342 species have been sighted. (In contrast, England—which is six times the size and home to many more bird-watchers—is home to only some

250 reported species.) Djibouti has its own species of bird as well, a kind of partridge called the Djibouti francolin. The species is currently endangered, with only approximately 1,500 francolins remaining. But the most impressive attraction Djibouti offers to bird-lovers is the annual migration of birds coming from Arabia, across the Bab el Mandeb, to Djibouti and the rest of Africa. Every year, from September to November an estimated quarter of a million birds fly this route as they head south for the winter. Serious bird-watchers come from all over the world every year to watch this spectacle.

Finally, Djibouti boasts a rich undersea life that is slowly but surely luring intrepid scuba divers from around the world. The government hopes to develop the scuba diving industry as a source of tourist revenue. Djibouti's unique location between the Indian Ocean and the Red Sea means that its marine life is very diverse, enriched by species only seen in the Gulf of Tadjoura. This part of the sea is graced with huge expanses of coral, so plentiful that it has even been used as a building material! The coral attracts dozens upon dozens of fish, such as angel and butterfly fish, appreciated for their beauty as well as their taste and price value on the world market. Huge schools of snapper, sturgeon, and barracuda pass regularly through Djibouti's water, making it not just a scuba diver's paradise, but a fisherman's as well.

A tower with architectural carvings, located in Aksum, Ethiopia. The kingdom of Aksum expanded from Ethiopia and incorporated the territory of Djibouti in the first century B.C. Over the course of the next 1,000 years, this great trading empire had several official religions, including Christianity and Islam.

History

Djibouti is one of the world's youngest independent republics, but the region itself is hardly new. In fact, historic Djibouti and the surrounding region is where some scientists believe human history began.

The Great Rift Valley, the huge geological feature that slices the continent of Africa almost in two, extends from the valley of the Jordan River to South Africa, with a few breaks in its stretch. If you were to look at a **topographical** map of the continent, the valley is clearly visible, and gives the impression that someone stabbed Egypt with a giant knife a billion years ago and dragged it through thousands of miles of rock and soil before finally pulling it out again in South Africa. And it is out of this dramatic feature, which sits to the west of Djibouti, that the earliest humans might have evolved. Those who believe that humankind originated here call it "the Cradle of Humanity."

Paleontologists gathered significant evidence about human origins with a discovery in Ethiopia in 1974 that was one of the most famous scientific breakthroughs of the 20th century. In the Hadar Valley of Ethiopia, which lies in the Afar Triangle, scientist Donald Johanson discovered a skull that was at the time the oldest human-like remains ever found. Later investigations showed her to be a female, after which she was christened "Lucy" by Johanson, the world press, and the scientific community. Believed to have lived 3.2 million years ago, Lucy's discovery stunned scientists all over the world; no one had before seen the remains of a creature so old yet so advanced. Lucy was classified as an *Australopithecus*, not a *Homo sapiens*, the scientific nomenclature for modern humans. The distinction between the two species acknowledged that Lucy had a brain the size of a chimpanzee's, but also that she and the rest of her community in East Africa were able to walk upright and use tools—two capabilities that marked a significant step forward in the history of human evolution.

Since the discovery of Lucy, scientists have begun to turn their attention to other sites in the Afar Triangle, including locations in Djibouti. It is here that scientists have discovered some of the very earliest examples of organized farming. The period that these humans lived in was another important stage in human history. Once humans were able to settle down and farm a piece of land, they had more time to develop all sorts of new technologies and skills. To modern people these developments may seem primitive, but they also paved the way for many subsequent forms of technology.

In 1984, conclusive proof that Djibouti was an early site of human settlement was discovered. At the town of Hara Ide, a team of French researchers discovered remains of *Homo sapiens* and *Homo erectus* (an ancestor of modern man) dating back 1.5 million years. And in the late 1980s, at the remote Lac Abbe (Lake Abbe) on the border with Ethiopia, an area described as a "slice of the moon on the crust of the earth," scientists made more discoveries of prehistoric settlements. Among the most important things dicovered were gigantic 4,000-year-old millstones (circular stones used for the grinding of grains) made from basalt, as well as tools made of **obsidian**, both of which suggests the practice of agriculture and settled development in the region during the Neolithic era (circa 8000 B.C.–1500 B.C.). Paleontologists continue to work toward discovering what other secrets Djibouti's soil may still hold, and to sort through many basic questions about how the region's earliest inhabitants lived.

THE KINGDOM OF AKSUM

Djibouti, as a discrete piece of territory with its own government, is a relatively new entity. Long before becoming an independent state, Djibouti was a part of the ancient Ethiopian kingdom of **Aksum**, an early African empire established in the second century B.C. and which lasted, in one form or another, for well over a thousand years. The Aksumites originally lived in the Ethiopian highlands, but through growth and conquest eventually took over much of the surrounding region and even held territory across the Red Sea on the Arabian Peninsula. By the first century B.C., the land we now call Djibouti had been absorbed into the kingdom of Aksum, an entirely predictable event, as the region was located directly to Aksum's south.

The era of the Aksum kingdom is a fascinating chapter in African history. Because of its central position in the trading routes between Arabia, India, Africa, and Europe, the kingdom grew fantastically wealthy. Even in its early days, Greek and Roman writers gave testimony to the Aksum kingdom's great prosperity and wealth. In its years as a Christian state, the kingdom's riches became the stuff of legend. As late as the Middle Ages many Europeans believed it to be the home of the Christian king, Prester (Priest) John, who according to myths possessed a vast fortune of gold.

The story of Christianity in Aksum is an interesting one, especially as it relates to the arrival and eventual spread of Islam in the region. Although it was an especially diverse kingdom, with at one time minorities of Nubians (ancestors of modern-day Egyptians and Sudanese), Jews, and even Buddhists living in its cities, Aksum eventually became Christian. Before they were brought under an official Christian state, however, Aksum's citizens adhered to a **polytheistic** religion related to the pre-Islamic religions of the Arabian Peninsula. All that changed in the fourth century A.D., when a Syrian bishop named Frumentius converted Emperor Ezana to Christianity. But the Christianity of the Aksumites, though fairly close to modern Christian practice in Ethiopia and Eritrea, differs from the Christian faith practiced by most of the world today.

One primary difference between this form of Christianity and the orthodox faith relates to doctrine: mainstream Christians believed and still believe that Christ had two natures (human and divine). The Christian Aksums, however, testified to the **Monophysite** (*mono* = "single," *physite* = "nature") doctrine of Jesus Christ, which meant they regarded Christ as being entirely divine. This heresy led to a major division in the religion during the first millennium.

The other major difference between the sects was a cultural one. Because the Christians of Aksum spoke a Semitic language (its present-day version, Amharic, is still spoken today in Ethiopia), they traced their origins all the way back to King David of the Old Testament. By extension, they saw themselves as the official inheritors of the new covenants of the New Testament. Today, the Ethiopian Church still claims to hold the Ark of the Covenant, in which the Hebrews kept the Ten Commandments written on stone tablets. Scholars have requested to see the ark in order to test the Church's claims, but only a special guardian of the Ark is permitted to see the sacred relic.

A sculpture relief of the Ark of the Covenant, which appears among the ruins of a synagogue in Israel. The Ark, recorded in the Old Testament as the place where the Ten Commandments are stored, is revered in Jewish and Christian tradition. The Ethiopian Church, which claims descent as far back as King David, has stated that it guards the Ark in one of its churches.

THE ARRIVAL OF ISLAM

While Aksum was growing and thriving as a Christian trading empire, events across the Red Sea were taking place that would threaten the kingdom. Around A.D. 570, the prophet Muhammad was born in the town of **Mecca** on the Arabian Peninsula. The influence Muhammad had on his followers and subsequent events would lead to the restructuring of a number of African kingdoms.

Orphaned as a child, Muhammad had an uncle who took him into his home and trained him as a merchant and a trader. When he was 25, Muhammad married the widow Khadija, who had been left wealthy by her first husband. Of the six children that she and Muhammad had, only their four daughters survived, the two boys dying in infancy. Despite these tragedies, the couple enjoyed a very comfortable existence, with great prosperity and respect among their friends in Mecca.

After some 15 years, however, Muhammad began to hear voices and experience visions. A deep spiritual unrest followed and he went in search of solitude so that he might better understand what was happening to him. He found a cave in the mountains above Mecca, where the angel Gabriel appeared and told him to pass on the wisdom and teachings of Allah (God).

Others joined Muhammad when they heard his recitations of the angel's visit and the teachings that the angel commanded him to

The prophet Muhammad receives Allah's holy word in this engraving. In the beginning of the seventh century, Muhammad preached Allah's message, which became known as the Qur'an. Islam was born and eventually spread from the Arabian Peninsula to Djibouti, though many Christians of the Aksum Empire resisted conversion for centuries.

begin. His recitations became the **Qur'an** (or Koran), the holy book of Islam. The new faith was quickly growing, and it was so eagerly embraced by those who heard it that the local authorities soon felt their security was threatened.

Sometime in 622, Muhammad left Mecca for **Medina** (in Arabia), where the new religion became an even stronger force. Muhammad and his followers began sacred Muslim traditions, such as praying in the direction of the **Ka'aba** stone in Mecca, which was first held sacred by the non-Muslim tribes of Arabia but eventually became the holiest site of Islam. At this point the new faith of Islam was born. Muhammad would live only 10 years after he dictated the Qur'an, but the seeds of Islam as an expansionist religion were planted. His followers supported themselves and their faith by warring on traveling caravans of non-believers. Perhaps Muhammad's beliefs would have died with him in 632 had it not been for the devotion of his followers and their newly instituted system of caliphs (Arabic for "deputies of the prophet"). This hierarchy allowed for a continual, stable chain of command for followers of the faith; thus organized, these Arabian Muslims could make war on neighboring tribes until they had forcibly converted not just the Arabian Peninsula but empires like Persia (now Iran) to Islam.

But while Islam enjoyed a rapid rise over a few centuries that brought the new faith quite literally to the doorstep of Europe (for a time, even Spain was held by the Moors of North Africa), the kingdom of Aksum avoided forced conversion for a long time. (Its stamina against the conquest perhaps resulted from the popularity of a legend that Muhammad had found sanctuary in modern-day Ethiopia after fleeing persecution in Arabia. Historians believe that the stories of the Aksums' kindness toward Muhammad convinced Muslims to extend mercy to these non-believers). Eventually, however, the Qur'an succeeded in making headway in the region. Continuing the tradition of their non-Islamic ancestors, the recently converted

Muslim Arabs continued to trade all along the Red Sea coast, including the area of Djibouti. There they settled and developed many port towns in the ninth century along what is now the country's coastline. A certain peace seemed to prevail, but soon religious practice would be changed in the entire region forever.

In 975, Muslims advanced on the kingdom of Adal, which was Aksum's neighboring state, situated in present-day Somalia. The Muslims conquered Zeila, Adal's main port town, just 40 miles (64 km) east of the present-day Djibouti border. Their success was primarily due to the Aksum kingdom being distracted by the separate invasions of pagan warriors. The victory over Zeila set the stage for Djibouti's fall to the Muslim conquerors, although the subsequent mass conversion of Christians to Islam occurred over a long period, in some areas taking centuries to complete.

Although the introduction of Islam to Djibouti was hardly a smooth transition, it was not long before a stabilizing force came to Djibouti in the form of the Ottoman Empire, a vast Muslim kingdom that lasted from the late 13th to the early 20th century. Having swept through modern-day Turkey (then Byzantium, the eastern part of the Roman Empire) and the city of Constantinople (now Istanbul), the Ottoman Empire took Egypt in 1517 and spread its influence down the eastern coast of North Africa and through the Arabian Peninsula. During most of the Ottomans' reign, regions along the empire's outskirts—including the land that became Djibouti and the surrounding areas—were generally Ottoman in name only. Sultans representing the empire collected taxes for the Ottomans, but the empire's involvement in government was minimal.

The Ottomans were known, among other things, for their military prowess and vast influence; however, their power became too unwieldy. They were eventually threatened most by the major European powers, which since the 15th century had undergone an expansion unrivalled in the world's history. It was not long before the militarily efficient Western nations picked off the Ottoman Empire's possessions one by one, and set their eyes on—among the many spoils of their victory—northern Africa. Most possessions were acquired after the Ottoman's devastating losses in World War I, but Europe had become involved in North Africa decades earlier.

THE BIRTH OF FRENCH SOMALILAND

In modern times, the most important improvement of the trade channel between the Red Sea and the Indian Ocean was the construction of the Suez Canal, which opened up land dividing the Red Sea and the Mediterranean. Construction of the canal began in 1859 and ended 10 years later. The two most dominant powers at the time, the British and the French, wanted control of parts of this region, primarily to facilitate the developing trade. With Italy, Belgium, and Germany, Britain and France were all playing the "Great Game," the object of which was to see who could add the most African territories to their empires in the shortest time. And Djibouti, with its prime location, was a prize, despite the fact that it was not an economically rich place.

For a while, it looked as if Britain were destined to win the prize. With Britain's extensive holdings along the Arabian side of the Red Sea, including the Yemeni port of Aden, as well as much of the Somali coast, it seemed all but a foregone conclusion. But the French were able to make a last-minute play for the land that would become Djibouti, and wound up purchasing the land in 1862 from local sultans representing the Ottoman Empire. (The territory they purchased was larger than the Djibouti of today; it was later shrunk under an agreement with the Ethiopians.) Thus was born French Somaliland (which became the Territory of Afars and Issas, then finally the Republic of Djibouti). The French made their first settlements in French Somaliland at the town of Obock. In 1892, after looking for a better port from which to reach the Red Sea, they moved their capital south to the port city of Djibouti town, founded in 1888.

One of the first things that the French did when they settled Djibouti town was to begin constructing a railroad that would stretch into the highlands of Ethiopia to that country's new capital, Addis Ababa. An efficient means of transport was key to the continuing development of French Somaliland; East African traders had plied the route between Ethiopia and the Djibouti coast for centuries, but goods now had to move more quickly. It took 20 years, but what became the Franco-Ethiopian Railroad in 1917 proved to be a great economic success for its planners.

As a French colony, Djibouti struggled to attain stability. During the first half of the 20th century, it found itself once again in the midst of the great powers—some battling for supremacy, others for survival. Soon after the fascist leader Benito Mussolini ascended to power in 1925, he made the acquisition of Ethiopia a primary goal. *Il Duce* (the Leader), as he was called by his adoring followers, was determined to participate in the scramble for African territory. It did not matter that there was little strategic or economic value in taking over Ethiopia; rather it simply repre-sented an opportunity for Italy to have her own overseas empire. Throughout the 1930s, French and Italian forces clashed over territories on a regular basis.

With the outbreak of World War II, French Somaliland experi-enced its own trauma. After France's rapid capitulation in 1940 to the invading German forces, its colony fell under the administra-tion of what was called the Vichy Government in France, which supported and followed the mandates of the Nazi regime. Consequently, Djibouti was subject to a British naval blockade between the fall of France until December 1942. The blockade was finally broken when Allied forces, along with Free French fighters, liberated Djibouti from Vichy-Nazi domination. In return for the

Italian dictator Benito Mussolini (left) and German dictator Adolf Hitler ride through the streets of Munich, Germany, in June 1940. The two leaders formed an alliance in 1936 that lasted through World War II. During Mussolini's campaign for territories in Africa, Italy clashed with France in the 1930s for control of Horn of Africa lands. France later fell to the Nazis and became Vichy France, putting Djibouti briefly under a different administration.

Allies' military support, a battalion of Djiboutian troops fought in the campaign to liberate France in 1944.

CRISIS AND INDEPENDENCE

With order restored to France, Djibouti was once again able to fulfill her role as something of a "service station" for ships moving through the Red Sea, especially for French ships making their way to Madagascar off Africa's eastern coast and Vietnam in the Far East. Djibouti City grew noticeably, and the colony was reorganized in 1957 as the French Territory of Afars and Issas (named after the two main tribes, one Ethiopian and the other Somali, who call the tiny country home). With its new identity, Djibouti enjoyed a great deal of local autonomy. In 1967, Djiboutian citizens voted 60 percent in favor of allowing the French to stay on as nominal rulers, partly in reward for their earlier show of leniency.

However, the second half of the 20th century was not the stable era that the people of Djibouti hoped it would be. Two events—the closure of the Suez Canal in 1967 and a series of regional wars— would keep Djibouti from enjoying a much-needed period of peace.

Since its construction, the Suez Canal has been one of the most important sea passages in the entire world. Although its usefulness has diminished somewhat in recent years with the latest generation of supertankers and other cargo ships too wide and too deep to pass through its locks, its existence has always contributed much to Djibouti's livelihood. Without the trade passing through the

An Egyptian tank sits incapacitated in the Sinai desert after a successful Israeli attack during the 1967 Six-Day War. Djibouti did not fight in the war, though trade suffered greatly after sunken ships blocked the Suez Canal, shutting it down for eight years.

canal, far fewer ships would pass by Djibouti.

The Suez Canal was at the center of a global crisis in 1967 when Israel fought what was later called the Six-Day War against neighboring Arab countries, all of whom were geared for the destruction of the new Jewish state. But Israel turned the tables on the Arab world, destroying much of its combined air forces before they even got a chance to leave the ground in a stunning military victory that found the Jewish state in possession of the Sinai Peninsula as well. The war closed Suez Canal for eight years, costing Djibouti revenue and shutting down the port's usefulness as a way station for ships moving from the Mediterranean to the Indian Ocean.

But while the crises of the Middle East would have some effect on Djibouti's well-being, the conflicts of northern Africa would be a heavier burden on the world's newest independent nation.

INDEPENDENCE FOR DJIBOUTI

In 1967, Djiboutians voted to keep the French on as colonial leaders; by 1977, Djibouti was one of the very few foreign-held pieces of land remaining on the entire continent of Africa. But during that year the government decided to begin a new era of independence.

On the night of June 27, the French tri-colored flag was furled, and the new flag of Djibouti was raised over the country. American journalist David Lamb, an accomplished reporter based in Africa, describes the event in *The Africans*:

> There was no great sense of excitement on that June evening in 1977. . . . Several hundred chairs were lined up near the piers for the ceremony and a handful of buildings were whitewashed at the last minute. The new airport passenger terminal opened and the La Siesta hotel put up a "No vacancy" sign. The French aircraft carrier *Foch* anchored a few miles out to sea in the unlikely event an evacuation of the expatriates would be necessary. . . . There was a shooting outside the barbed-wire perimeter that claimed one life when something called the Front for the Liberation of the Somali Coast—an outfit pledged to overthrowing the government that had

not yet even taken office—demanded permission to enter Djibouti. Gouled [Hassan Gouled Aptidon, the president-to-be] smoothed out the problem with some skillful negotiating, and most of the front's 3,000 members were left milling outside the barricade with their camels and guns. By eleven o'clock the invited guests were in their seats. The women, stout and big-chested, wore colorful print-cloth dresses, and the men sat glassy-eyed, chewing khat [*qat*], a narcotic weed imported from Ethiopia.

At precisely one minute past midnight, France's high commissioner, Camille d'Ornano, offered a crisp salute as the French tri-color [flag] was lowered and folded for the last time in Africa. Hassan Gouled Aptidon, who would move out of his little home and into the French governor's seaside mansion the next day, was now the president of Africa's fiftieth independent nation, the Republic of Djibouti. . . .

And so the former Territory of Afars and Issas became officially known as the Republic of Djibouti, an independent nation. Although they had no official government positions, French officials would still remain involved in Djibouti, providing economic assistance and military protection. At the helm of the new nation was Hassan Gouled Aptidon, a popular ruler who would manage to at least keep his country's head above water, though to accomplish this he upset some by using fairly brutal tactics.

But life as an independent nation did not start smoothly for this little port country. Just a month after Djibouti announced its independence, the bloody Ogaden War broke out, the culmination of hostilities between Somalia and Ethiopia that had been brewing for some time. The conflict was over the possession of the Ogaden region, which Somalian troops had entered and claimed in 1977. Somalia had gained independence in 1960, and in fighting the Ogaden War was looking to expand its borders. The war had several immediate effects on Djibouti—all of which were bad. First, the war, which was waged between two much-larger forces, threatened the survival of the newborn state—some historians would even say it nearly smothered the infant Djibouti in its crib. During its campaign against Ethiopia, Somalia considered incorporating Djibouti into the country. The annexation was logical, Somalia argued, since two-thirds of Djibouti's population traced its ancestry to various Somali tribes, or clans. The only factors keeping Djibouti from being gobbled up by its larger neighbor were the fierce desire of Djiboutians of all ethnic stripes to remain neutral and independent, and a garrison of 4,000 French troops.

The second and more devastating result of the war was that it absolutely ravaged the country's economy. Service on the all-important Addis Ababa–Djibouti rail line was interrupted during the war, which in turn disrupted almost all economic activity at the Djibouti port. No longer were ships coming in to take Ethiopian goods away

Passengers board a train in Djibouti headed to Addis Ababa, the capital of Ethiopia. This railroad, crossing 500 miles (805 km) of desert and rough terrain, facilitates Djiboutian trade. Many Ethiopian exports are shipped to the Djibouti port so that they can be delivered to the rest of the world.

for export; gone too were the port fees, duties, and levies that Djibouti relied upon. Following the 1977–78 War, won convincingly by Ethiopia, Djibouti was bankrupt in everything but its name. Then, nationwide poverty was made worse by the sudden influx of refugees streaming over the border. The refugees were trying to get away from what had become a treacherous zone in the global cold war between the two superpowers—United States and the former Soviet Union—and their African allies. Djibouti could ill afford to cope with such an onslaught of desperate people, especially under its existing economic circumstances.

A realignment of the region's politics followed the end of the Ogaden War, but Djibouti still faced unresolved issues. Ethnic tension, a reoccurring problem in Djibouti's history, still threatened to tear the country apart. As long as control of the nation was not evenly divided between the Issas and Afars, tensions would remain high.

President Aptidon was an Issa, but while in office he was aware of the need to not show favoritism to the Issas or the Afars. He might have learned a lesson from the post-independence

Djibouti leader Hassan Gouled Aptidon (1977–99) enjoyed a popular presidency despite the country's chronic ills—a struggling economy, the refugees from wars in Somalia and Ethiopia, and the regular clashes between the Issas and the minority Afar clan.

experiences of several countries in Africa: in many cases,
newly installed leaders
showed too much favoritism
to members of their own tribe
or clan, and in so doing
helped cause either civil wars
or the toppling of their own
regimes. Although no one had
any doubt that the Issas had
the upper hand in govern-

Djibouti was the last country on the continent of Africa to become independent, though in 1979, two years after Djibouti became an official republic, Rhodesia (now Zimbabwe) briefly reverted to rule under a British governor.

ment, Aptidon started out with a strategy to keep the people
pacified, appointing a cabinet and a staff that were reasonably
integrated between his own clansmen and Afars. But the harmo-
ny would not last for long.

The Afars and Issas have never seen eye to eye on many issues
in Djibouti, and the enmity between them seems as old as the
hills. So in 1978 it was not a surprise when Aptidon's government
experienced the first of many ethnic crises, with the new president
kicking out Afar cabinet members and prime ministers on two
occasions.

Other pressing issues during Aptidon's years were not the
outcome of ethnic tension, but poverty. Not counting refugees,
Djibouti had a population of around 450,000 when it won its independence, and most of them lived in Djibouti City—typically in vast
shantytowns and squatters' camps on the city's outskirts.

Even though the departure of the French meant that there
were now openings in the civil service and in other prestigious
professions, the vast majority of Djiboutians had either to hope for
employment at the port or along the 62 miles (100 km) of railroad
track leading from the port to the Ethiopian border. Those who
couldn't find jobs in these two fields, or land the few available

positions in the civil service, had to simply scratch whatever farming income they could out of the country's arid climate. A high cost of living, combined with accusations that government aid and subsidized housing programs were favoring the Issas, would contribute to the Afars' growing discontent over the next decade.

Meanwhile, Aptidon continued his long stretch as president. In 1981 he banned all opposition political parties and won election to a six-year term, and won again in 1987. Despite the suppression of opposition groups, the 1980s was a decade of relative peace for Djibouti, with the country's citizens working to get back on their feet. However, the next decade would pose a whole new series of challenges.

THE AFAR UPRISING

In late 1991, war broke out between the Afars and the Issas in what would be called the Afar Uprising, the result of tensions that had been building up since before Djibouti claimed its independence. For three years, fighting raged between government forces and Afar rebels, killing thousands of people and displacing many more. The fighting completely destabilized a country committed to making the most of its tough circumstances. According to the *Horn of Africa Bulletin*, in the country's northern regions, where many Djiboutians struggle to raise livestock, rain did not fall for an entire year. Within six months, half of the country's animal stocks died.

Compounding the crisis were the killings, destruction of property, forced migrations of Djiboutians, and a slew of other human rights' abuses the government committed against Afar rebels. These abuses caused aid from Western countries to dry up just as the nation was experiencing a catastrophic drought. In 1994, it was not hard to see that Djibouti was in a precarious position. At the end of that year, a peace accord was finally signed with the rebels; one of the most important terms of the accord was that Afar leaders

Iraqi president Saddam Hussein delivers a public statement in Baghdad
in August 2002. After Saddam ordered Iraqi forces to invade neighboring
Kuwait in 1990, President Aptidon allowed French and U.S. forces to set
up operations in Djibouti. The country's assistance helped improve the
government's public image, which suffered from brutal counterattacks
ordered against Afar rebels during the 1991 uprising.

received a place in government.

At this time, perhaps the only thing that redeemed Djibouti in the
eyes of the West in general and France in particular was its
participation in the 1991 Persian Gulf War between Iraq and a U.S.-
led coalition. Although Aptidon told his people that he was against a
military strike against Iraqi president Saddam Hussein, who had
recently rolled his tanks into neighboring Kuwait, he also allowed the
French to build up their military forces in the country in preparation
for a strike on Iraq, and in addition allowed American naval vessels
access to the port. Also, in a canny maneuver he negotiated for
Djibouti to be paid for the assistance it provided to Saudi Arabia, at
the time Saddam's next possible target. As part of the agreement,
Saudi Arabia agreed to pay for the renovation and modernization of
Djibouti's port.

Ismael Omar Guelleh replaced Hassan Gouled Aptidon as president of Djibouti in May 1999. In accordance with campaign promises, Guelleh has worked toward more peace resolutions in war-torn Somalia. He also has maintained positive relations with Western powers, particularly during the U.S.-led "war on terrorism," which began in late 2001.

Although the peace accords of 1994 announced an end to civil war in Djibouti, there would be sporadic outbreaks in the years since. The country would remain unstable in the latter half of that decade. While independent and opposition political parties had been legalized, government leaders struggled to solve its many problems. Relations between the Afars and the Issas still had not improved, social unrest was always imminent, and the economy was teetering on collapse. People who worked for or depended on the government would receive their paychecks months late. With the country's problems hanging over Aptidon, the president decided against running in the next election, but before leaving office he would have to navigate the country through yet another regional crisis.

In 1998, war broke out between Ethiopia and Eritrea. Five years earlier, Eritrea had won independence from Ethiopia, but a small piece of land on the border remained in dispute. The war, which lasted over two years, killed some 70,000 people and displaced many more, a good portion of whom wound up in Djibouti's refugee camps. However, though Djibouti was burdened with even more refugees, it also gained from the spoils of the Ethiopia-Eritrea war: with Eritrea now obstructing its enemy's access to the

Red Sea, Ethiopia had to rely entirely on Djibouti's port and railroad line. As a result, Djibouti gained greater port revenue, employment, and trade.

The 22-year rule of Hassan Gouled Aptidon finally came to an end with the free and multi-party elections of 1999. The candidate, Ismael Omar Guelleh, ran on a platform that included helping next-door neighbor Somalia, which at this point had fallen apart and was in the hands of rival warlords with their own private armies. Guelleh sought to pull Somalia out of its crisis while reconciling Djibouti under the idea of a "civil society" and integrating the region's economies into a single common market. He won the 1999 election easily with 74 percent of the vote. The fact that Guelleh was Aptidon's nephew and his main advisor for over 20 years probably did not hurt the results. However, international election monitors reported that the electoral contest was conducted openly, and that inconsistencies were in most cases solely due to technical problems.

Djibouti has remained relatively stable since Guelleh's ascent to power. Guelleh's presidency is reminiscent of Aptidon's in how he has managed the country's international affairs, specifically with the assistance Djibouti has provided to the West. The country agreed to play its part in the U.S.-led "war on terrorism," which began following the 2001 terrorist attacks in New York and Washington. In the spring of 2002, American and German troops were stationed in Djibouti, along with a contingent of attack helicopters. In 2003, the American forces there prepared for deployment in a war in Iraq, which began in March of that year. Guelleh has skillfully justified the presence of the foreign troops to his people, who hope that this new relationship will mean more aid and employment. Already there is some sign of that happening, as the U.S. government is presently considering an increase of foreign aid to Djibouti.

Muslims pray at the Ka'aba in Mecca. Believers from Djibouti and around the world arrive to Mecca to satisfy the requirements of the hajj, or pilgrimage. Those who successfully make the journey earn the title of *Hajji*.

Politics, Religion and the Economy

Djibouti's political system, based on the French model of a republic, is a legacy of the colonial era. There is a president and prime minister who serve for six-year terms, and a legislature and a single-house Chamber of Deputies, consisting of 65 members, who are elected by popular vote and serve five-year terms. Further down the ladder, Djibouti also has five administrative regions, and a French-style system of civil law that incorporates Islamic law and tradition. There is also a judicial system, although most foreign observers do not consider it a legitimately independent body.

Djiboutian politics has greatly suffered from the rivalries between the Afars and Issas, their disputes often boiling over with tragic results. The most effective stabilizing force has been the party known as the *Rassemblement Populaire le Progres* (RPP); in English, the "Popular Rally for Progress."

Established in 1979, the party was specifically designed to resolve disputes between Afars and Issas. At the time, disputes were clearly imminent, as Djibouti had at an Issa president, Hassan Gouled Aptidon, and an Afar prime minister, Ahmed Dini Ahmed. Aptidon, who was to lead Djibouti through two decades of regional and internal strife, was a canny leader who nearly always maintained a balance in his government between members of his own tribe and the Afars. Unfortunately, the harsh methods that he used to accomplish this balance were not always well received by the people of Djibouti, and in 1980, a disgruntled Dini and several other Afars walked out of the government. In response, Aptidon declared the RPP the country's only legal party the following year. Not surprisingly, the RPP won subsequent elections in 1982 and 1987.

By 1990, the situation had gotten out of control. No matter how cleverly Aptidon played both sides of the fence and kept his twin constituencies from going for each others' throats, he could not keep the lid on Djibouti's ethnic tensions any longer. In 1991 the Afar rebellion broke out, as people both inside and outside Djibouti called for an end to the one-party system and the legalization of political opposition parties. The government cracked down hard on

Former Djibouti prime minister Ahmed Dini Ahmed, an Afar, resigned from his position in 1980, complaining that President Aptidon showed favoritism to Issas tribe members. Following his departure Ahmed became leader of *Front pour la Restauration de l'Unité et de la Démocratie* (FRUD), a rebel group that in 1991 helped begin the three-year-long Afar Uprising.

The flag of Djibouti was officially hoisted on June 27, 1977, to mark the country's independence. The blue stripe represents the Issas clan, the green stripe the Afars, and the red star is a symbol of unity.

the Afar rebels in Djibouti town, and an armed insurgency was launched against the government, led by none other than the former prime minister, Ahmed Dini.

For a while, Dini found success as leader of the Afar group, *Front pour la Restauration de l'Unité et de la Démocratie* (more commonly known for its acronym, FRUD). The rebellion spread fast throughout the traditional Afar tribal areas in the northern part of the country. After four months of much bloodshed and too many casualties, France stepped in as a peace broker and initiated talks between the two sides. In 1992, Djibouti's government hoped to officially end the conflict with a completely new constitution, approved by a popular referendum (vote by the entire citizenry). The constitution supported a more democratic government by allowing other opposition parties to operate. (The arrangement, however, turned out to be not as democratic as it promised: only four parties were legalized, and through a series of maneuverings, Aptidon ensured that the new constitution reserved most of the power for the president.)

The new legislation also failed to put a final end to the Afar Uprising. It was not until the middle of 1993 that government forces were able to recapture much of the territory they had lost in the north to the insurgents, at which point the FRUD movement was both defeated and divided. Later, in 1994, FRUD signed a peace accord with the Aptidon government; two of its members joined the cabinet.

Aptidon's nephew and handpicked successor, Ismael Omar Guelleh, replaced the president in 1999 at the end of his final six-year term. Guelleh had been the cabinet director for two decades, and in the multi-party elections he took the reins of power in Djibouti with a healthy percentage of the vote, beating the only other candidate for the position, Moussa Ahmed Idriss of the *Opposition djiboutienne unifée* (ODU).

No parties boycotted or protested the 1999 elections, which was surprising for a country in which one party had for so many years kept a tight-fisted grip on power. In addition, international observers believe that the voting was carried out in a fair manner without interference from the government. The multi-party national-al assembly elections of 2003, held in January, also proved to be a democratic affair, according to spectators.

Fair elections do not necessarily equate a free state, however. Since Guellah's ascension in 1999, international observers have been critical of his conduct, especially of his violations of citizens' rights and censorship of the press. In the United States and other free countries, almost everyone takes for granted that a newspaper can publish whatever it wants about the government (as long as it does not contain slander or libel), but during Guellah's presidency, Djiboutians have not enjoyed freedom of the press. The government controls the country's principal newspaper, *La Nation de Djibouti*.

Furthermore, the government of Djibouti does not respect the rights of people to speak out against it, and people who criticize the government have been known to wind up in jail for years without ever hearing so much as the charge filed against them. In its 2000 report on human rights in Djibouti, the U.S. State Department stated:

> The Government's human rights record remained poor . . . and serious problems remain. . . . The Government continued to harass and intimidate political opponents, and to arrest and detain persons arbitrarily. Prolonged detention and incommunicado [solitary] detention remained problems. The judiciary is not independent of the executive and does not ensure citizens' due process.

RELIGION

Djibouti has been an Islamic territory for at least 1,000 years. But what does it mean to follow Islam—and specifically, what does it mean in Djibouti, a country with a unique Islamic history?

Islam grew out of the Arabian Peninsula over 1,300 years ago, and today almost 1 billion people are Muslims. It shares company with Christianity and Judaism as one of the three major monotheistic religions (faiths that believe in one god). As such, there are many similarities in doctrine and belief between Islam and the other religions, but there also visible differences.

The central prayer and statement of belief for Muslims is a simple one known as the ***Shahada***, which states: "There is no god but Allah, and Muhammad is His Prophet." The word *Allah* literally translates as "the one God." Muslims include several texts in their holy literature, including the Old Testament scriptures, but they believe that the Qur'an is the holiest. Its authority lies in the fact that it was dictated by Muhammad, whom Muslims regard as the greatest and last of all prophets. Muslims also include the teachings of Jesus in their doctrine, believing that he was a great prophet, though not the Son of God as Christians affirm.

Muslims share with the monotheistic religions a belief in angels,

An elaborately decorated page from a Qur'an manuscript, dating from the 12th century. Unlike the Bible, a holy text that is written by several authors, the Qur'an is believed to be the pure, untouched word of Allah.

which stems originally from Muhammad's original vision of the angel Gabriel. And like Christians, Muslims look forward to a final "day of judgment" on which the world as we know it ends and the wicked and the just get their ultimate and deserved reward.

But this is basically where the similarities end. Muslims subscribe to the five pillars of Islam, the first of which is to believe and recite the *Shahada*. The remaining four pillars are as follows:

Salat (prayer): One of the first things that catches the attention of first-time visitors to any Muslim city is the regular call to prayer, the first of which occurs before dawn. These calls come five times a day and are broadcast from mosques, or Muslim houses of worship, and remind all Muslims to stop what they are doing, bow down in the direction of Mecca, and say their devotions. Even if Muslims are not within earshot of a mosque, they must still pray five times a day. (Often, though, Muslims in Djibouti and elsewhere do not interrupt their daily routine and instead "make up" their prayers later at home.)

Zakat (charity): In some ways, this is similar to the guidelines of the many branches of Protestant Christianity that encourage regular "tithing," or donation of a fixed portion of one's income. For Muslims, charity is one of the highest virtues, whether it involves giving to a poor beggar or helping a traveler who needs a place to stay for the night. And while the doctrine that people should give a fixed proportion of their incomes to the poor is considered to have a purifying effect on the givers, it also has a practical benefit. With every Muslim required to give money to the poor, the practice—at least in theory—eliminates the need for social welfare in Islamic societies.

Sawm (fasting): Along with giving to charity, Muslims are also required to fast regularly, as the practice is considered to be purifying. During **Ramadan**, the ninth month of the Islamic calendar (which is based on the cycles of the moon), Muslims are supposed to avoid eating, drinking, or smoking tobacco from sunup to sundown. As one might imagine, this can be a difficult task in many of the hot, desert regions where Islam is practiced; most of the faithful stay inside all day and then break the fast at night by enjoying great feasts with their families.

Hajj (the pilgrimage to Mecca): This is the final, and perhaps most central, pillar of Islamic faith. Once in his life, every male Muslim must—if he is financially and physically capable—make a pilgrimage to the holy cities of Mecca and Medina. Women, too, can make the pilgrimage, but it is not required of them. Every year millions of Muslims make the journey at an appointed time to pray at a series of holy sites in an impressive display of humanity and devotion. It is considered a great achievement for a Muslim to make the pilgrimage, and those who have completed it often wear white skullcaps and take the honorific title of *Hajji*.

As a religion that encompasses so many aspects of the believer's life, from sunup to sundown and beyond, Islam exerts a powerful force on those who embrace it. However, Islam in Djibouti, which is practiced by an estimated 96 percent of the population, takes its own unique form. Perhaps because of the country's exposure to so many different cultures over the centuries, or perhaps because of the strong pulls of tribal loyalty that often take precedence over religious commitments, Djibouti's practice of the religion does not attract the extreme interpretations one finds in other Muslim countries like Iran or Saudi Arabia. For example, unlike many other Muslim countries, Islamic law in Djibouti—known as **Sharia**—is restricted to family and civil matters, and competes with traditional tribal law, known as **xeer**, for jurisdiction within the French-influenced state legal system.

This does not mean Djiboutian society practices complete tolerance, especially toward women, who still face official discrimination under the local form of *Sharia* and are not even allowed to travel without a male relative. Yet there are no formal religious police units enforcing Islamic dress codes as there are in other Muslim countries. When authorities do enforce the precepts of *Sharia*, citizens often find ways to evade the law. For example, when fundamentalists tried in 1995 to prohibit bars from serving alcohol, the offending institutions simply started classifying themselves as restaurants to avoid prosecution.

The nomadic people of Djibouti's hinterlands practice a form of Islam that is even further removed from orthodoxy. While they are all professed Muslims and exhibit great reverence, their faith remains a mixture of Islam and ancient tribal religion dating back to the time before monotheistic worship. The main feature of these ancient practices, which are followed by both Afars and Issas, is an intense devotion—bordering on worship—to dead ancestors, many of whom are considered saints.

RELIGIOUS CELEBRATIONS

Djibouti's biggest celebrations of the year focus on the Islamic holidays that are based on the Muslim calendar, which coincides with the cycles of the moon rather than the Western 365-day calendar. Subsequently, the dates of these events vary from year to year. The most important religious observances for Muslims in Djibouti and the rest of the world are Ramadan, Eid al-Fitr, and Eid al-Adha.

Ramadan is a month during which Muslims fast from sunrise to sunset. The fast dictates that they abstain from all liquids and food, as well as smoking. These restrictions are based on the belief that the spirit can be purified by denying the body material and worldly pleasure. Along with denying themselves food and drink, Muslims must also behave in a spiritual manner. According to Islamic doctrine, all the good done in a day's fasting can be undone by gossiping or spreading false rumors, or simply acting in a covetous manner.

Though most religions have a ritual annual fast and period of self-denial—such as Yom Kippur in Judaism or Lent in Christianity—Ramadan is one of the more extreme periods of the three faiths. People in Djibouti, like most Muslims, treat this time of abstinence with great respect. Streets are relatively empty, as many people use the

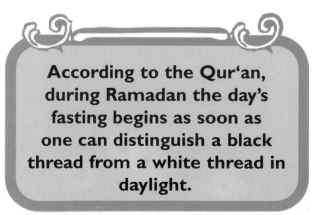

According to the Qur'an, during Ramadan the day's fasting begins as soon as one can distinguish a black thread from a white thread in daylight.

The parts of a slaughtered sheep lie on the ground during a celebration of Eid al-Adha, a Muslim holiday of sacrifice. Muslims are required to save a portion of the slaughtered animal for the poor. Djiboutians practice the sacrifice as a way to remember the sacrifice the patriarch Abraham intended for his son Ishmael.

time for meditation and serious concentration on the Qur'an. This quiet period lasts the entire day; when night arrives, families gather for a large dinner.

Perhaps the most important festival in the Islamic and Djiboutian calendar is the celebration feast of Eid al-Fitr at the end of Ramadan. Lasting three days, the joyous celebration is in spirit much like Christmas in the West. It is considered obligatory for Muslims to give to the poor during this time, and parents usually give children presents and new clothes.

The other great festival of the Islamic calendar is Eid al-Adha ("Festival of the Sacrifice"), commemorating the Old Testament prophet Abraham and his willingness to sacrifice his son Ishmael to God. Muslims in many countries, including Djibouti, follow the tradition faithfully, and some families sacrifice an animal, such as a live goat, in commemoration of the event. Today, the family who will eat the animal does not typically perform the actual slaughter, since more and more Djiboutians live in cities where meat merchants carry out this function. The four-day festival occurs approximately two months and ten days after Eid al-Fitr. It also marks the last day of the hajj season.

ECONOMY

It is almost hard to believe how Djibouti survives with such a struggling economy. The average Djiboutian makes $1,300 a year, and the country suffers from a devastating 50-percent unemployment rate. If it were not for Djibouti's strategic location in the Red Sea, or the natural harbor that graces Djibouti town, it would have virtually no means of income. With droughts routinely ravaging the country, prospects for agriculture are scarce. Djibouti only has a grand total of 6,000 acres of arable land. For an illustration of just how hard-pressed Djibouti's farms are to feed its 470,000 people—in addition to its large refugee population—consider that the average American farm is 469 acres. In other words, Djibouti has about a dozen or so American farms' worth of cultivatable land.

Other factors, too, have conspired to keep Djibouti poor. The Afar Uprising, for example, delivered a serious blow to the economy. During that time, a bad situation turned for the worse as government expenditures skyrocketed to fight the insurgency, and foreign countries withheld their aid in protest of the government's response to the rebellion. Djibouti's agriculture produces barely any goods for export, despite the fact that a huge number of people work in that sector. There are few other natural resources, and though recent explorations have suggested that Djibouti may be sitting on some potentially valuable natural gas reserves, they have not yet been tapped.

Train passengers on the Addis Ababa–Djibouti line buy meat from vendors. Because Djiboutians deal with a lack of natural resources, they make good use of the rail line that brings Ethiopian goods such as meat, coffee, dried beans, and salt.

With all these factors working against Djibouti's economy, though, the government and the people continue to adapt for their survival. Djibouti makes good use of its railroad, which allows trade with Ethiopia; and the port of Djibouti, which grants access to the rest of the world. Using these two assets in tandem, Djibouti is able to eke out a role in the world economy.

Djibouti's export numbers prove how little revenue its few natural resources generate: exports to the United States average around a scant $100,000 per year, while imports average $26.6 million. Fortunately, neighboring Ethiopia is endowed with natural resources, and with the Addis Ababa–Djibouti railroad, Djibouti is able to profit from the shipping of Ethiopian goods such as coffee, dried beans, salt, and cereals to its port, from where they are exported. The Djiboutian industry benefits from a large community of expatriates, or foreigners living overseas, who bring their managing expertise as well as extra money to the country. Indeed, particularly in the years since the Afar Uprising, Djibouti has made excellent use of its port facilities. Lately Djibouti has brought in foreign managers from Dubai in the United Arab Emirates to further increase the efficiency of operations. Today the port is considered a major transshipment hub of the Red Sea, and it will mostly likely remain Djibouti's most valuable asset.

But the fact of the matter is that despite its strategic location, Djibouti cannot reliably sustain an economy of 470,000 people—plus a large number of refugees—on its own. Djibouti relies greatly on foreign aid, and thus is pressured to implement the economic reforms that large donor countries and organizations like the World Bank have petitioned for. Although the country has always had a

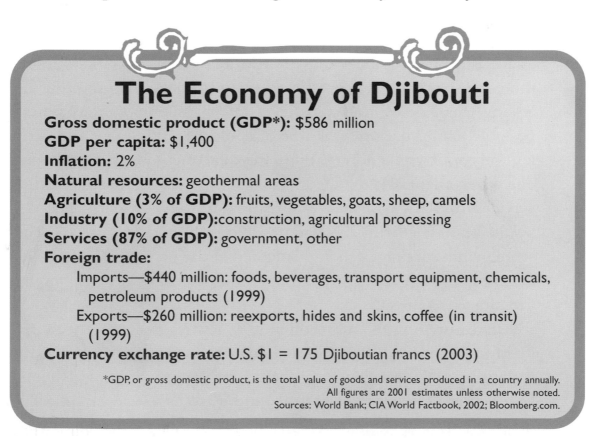

The Economy of Djibouti

Gross domestic product (GDP*): $586 million
GDP per capita: $1,400
Inflation: 2%
Natural resources: geothermal areas
Agriculture (3% of GDP): fruits, vegetables, goats, sheep, camels
Industry (10% of GDP): construction, agricultural processing
Services (87% of GDP): government, other
Foreign trade:
    Imports—$440 million: foods, beverages, transport equipment, chemicals, petroleum products (1999)
    Exports—$260 million: reexports, hides and skins, coffee (in transit) (1999)
Currency exchange rate: U.S. $1 = 175 Djiboutian francs (2003)

*GDP, or gross domestic product, is the total value of goods and services produced in a country annually.
All figures are 2001 estimates unless otherwise noted.
Sources: World Bank; CIA World Factbook, 2002; Bloomberg.com.

fairly liberal economy—with people free to start and operate businesses without undue interference from the government—its economic policies have only recently focused on getting the most out of its meager resources.

The most serious economic crisis of recent years occurred in 1996. After years of employing quick-fix solutions to economic problems, the government in Djibouti town finally announced the inevitable: the budget would have to be cut, and with it, services and payments to ordinary Djiboutians. The extremely unpopular decision was greeted with a general strike and protests in the streets. Later that same year, however, the government collaborated with France, the biggest aid contributor to Djibouti, and with international lending authorities at the World Bank and the IMF (International Monetary Fund) to find longer-term solutions to their financial woes.

As a result of these meetings, Djibouti was able to obtain loans and credits from France and the two lending organizations under the condition that the government was to make various reforms, among them de-centralizing the economy, taking whatever steps possible to improve livestock and agriculture production, and turning the country into a free-trade zone to attract foreign investment. The government also initiated a plan to privatize many state-owned services and turn them over to investors who—experts hoped—would be able to run them more efficiently and at a profit. This strategy has already been implemented at the port, which increased its handling capacity, though not as dramatically as foreign investors had hoped.

The future of Djibouti's economy, as always, rests on the stability of the Persian Gulf region. Periods of peace in the Gulf and the resolutions of the region's conflicts have helped preserve Djibouti as a center of free trade, banking, and services. However, following the September 2001 terrorist attacks on American soil, Djibouti has found itself in a different situation. The country's participation in U.S.-led military campaigns against terrorists and their allies will most likely help its economy. As part of its commitment to the international "war on terrorism," Djibouti has agreed to the stationing of U.S. armed forces on its soil. The Djibouti government hopes that American dollars spent by the American soldiers, as well as by the U.S. government to house and feed them, will give an extra boost to Djibouti's foreign earnings.

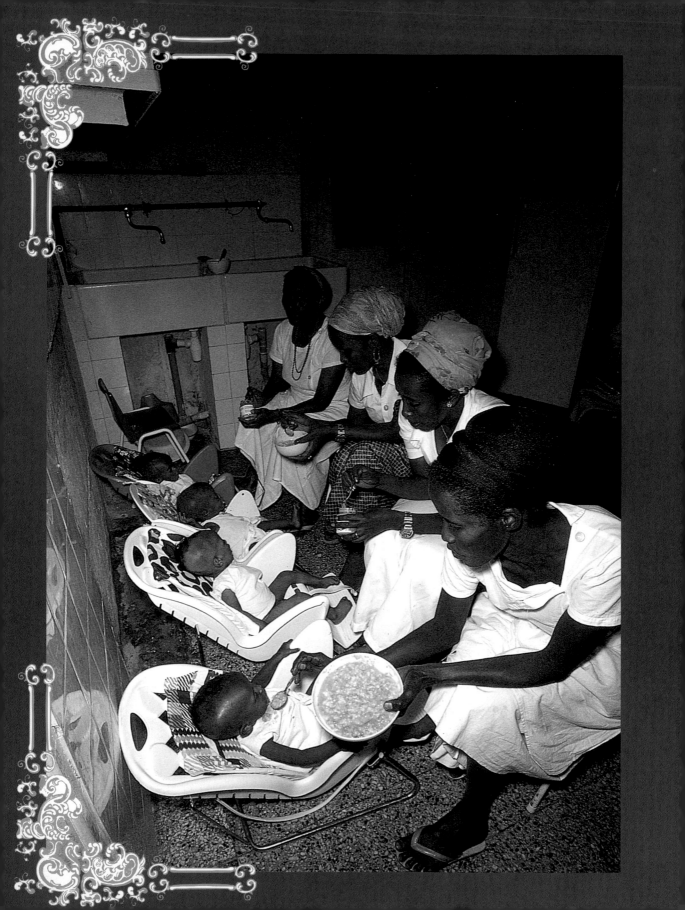

A group of Djiboutian women feed babies at a city hospital. The fertility rate is very high in Djibouti; with an expanding youth population, child heath care, education, and the economy remain central issues.

The People

What does it mean to be a Djiboutian? With tribal loyalty taking such precedence, the question does not have an easy answer. Many citizens consider themselves Afars and Issas first and Djiboutians second. The conflicting lifestyles of people in the cities and rural areas further complicate the idea of a national identity.

There are, however, a few elements that identify nearly all Djiboutians. Islam, for example, is extremely popular, with Muslims making up 96 percent of the population. Djiboutians also have their own unique pastimes and cultural practices, from their love of henna tattoos and body art to their fondness for chewing the narcotic leaf known as *qat*.

AFARS AND ISSAS

Besides the estimated 200,000 or so refugees living in the country at any one time or another, Djibouti's population is primarily a diverse group of Afars and Issas, and city and country dwellers. Of the population group that does not include the refugees, estimated at over 470,000 in 2002, approximately 60 percent are considered Issas, or Somali, and 35 percent are considered members of Afar, or Ethiopian, tribes. The remaining 5 percent is made of various minority groups who have settled in Djibouti over the years, including Arabs, Italians, and French people.

The population is growing at a rate of 2.6 percent, a rate that would be higher were it not for the country's startlingly high infant-mortality rate, which is the product of poverty and poor health care. Indeed, all Djiboutians suffer as a result of the country's poverty; everything from literacy rates to life expectancy are impeded by the country's chronic lack of funds and resources, despite the efforts of foreign powers to lend a hand.

There have always been tensions between the Afars and the Issas, although neither group has ever sought to return en masse to their ethnic homelands of Ethiopia and Somalia, as they have always kept a separate identity in Djibouti. The biggest problem facing the two groups is that many Afars have long believed that they are victims of discrimination. Despite the government's attempts at reconciliation, the Afars have felt their second-class status so keenly that they have sometimes resorted to open, armed rebellion, as in the Afar Uprising of the 1990s.

The tribal warfare tradition is deeply entrenched among the Afars and the Issas. (Some Afar men still file their teeth into fierce points as a display of their warrior heritage.) Although the two groups are thought to both descend from common ancestors, to speak languages that are fairly similar, and to organize their tribes and families in similar ways, they have participated in a legendary feud that goes back so far its origins are uncertain. Throughout the 19th century, Western travelers reported on the fierce fighting between the two groups, descriptions of which make the Afar

This map shows the distribution of people in Djibouti. Two-thirds of the population lives in the capital city, Djibouti.

Two Afar fighters display their swords. Comprising roughly one-third of Djibouti's population, the Afars have ancestral ties to Ethiopia. Their rivalry with the Issas is centuries old; the Afar Uprising, which began in 1991, damaged tribe relations for much of the 1990s.

Uprising of the early 1990s look calm by comparison. During a battle between the two tribes in 1935, 300 people were reported to have been killed in one assault.

The Afars are a nomadic people who are thought to have come down from the highlands of southeast Ethiopia centuries ago, bringing with them their unique nomadic lifestyle. In general, Afars tend to stay within their own subtribe, which is organized closely along male family lines. Within the Afars are two main classes of people, the *Asaimara*, or "Red Men," who constitute the tribe's nobility, and the *Adoimara*, or "White Men," who make up the peasant class and do not own property. In general, Afar nomads tend to keep to themselves and their group; even marriages are strictly controlled within the lines of class and tribe. The main occupations of the Afars—herding goats and camels and mining salt—suit their solitary lifestyle.

The Issas also lead a pastoral life, but organize themselves in a different fashion. For the Issas and other Somalis in Djibouti, loyalty rests on the **rer**, a significantly larger group than the sub-tribe of the Afars. The *rer* is a large congregation of families all claiming descent from the same male ancestor. Each *rer* is part of a larger tribe, with a leadership structure based on councils of male elders and advisors.

Despite the differences between the Afars and Issas, they both have a few fundamental things in common. Along with adhering to the precepts of Islam, the Afars and Issas believe strongly in the traditions of genealogy, or family ties. Class distinctions, practiced

An aerial view of Djibouti and its port. The large white building at the near end of the causeway is the president's residence; before independence, the building belonged to the French governor.

in both tribes, prohibit virtually any kind of upward mobility. In other words, a member of a lower class has very little chance to move out of it through marriage alliances or by other means.

A Djiboutian student finishes a class project. Many Djiboutian girls are taken out of school early in their childhood to take care of domestic duties. Child labor has long been prevalent in the country, cutting short the education of both boys and girls.

Both in town and in the remote parts of the country, it is common for Afars and Issas to live with their extended families. Generally, when a woman marries (usually in her late teens), she will move into the house of her husband, which often holds his entire extended family. Students who have moved to the city to study will most often stay with relatives rather than live on their own. Similarly, unmarried men and women generally don't live by themselves, but remain living with their extended families.

EDUCATION

More than 40 percent of the entire country's population is under age 14. Because the numbers of the country's youth are always expanding, education is as vital an issue as ever for Djibouti. Its government acknowledges that its citizens must be trained to be productive and also that, once they are trained, they enter a peaceful and stable environment in which their talents can be put to use.

Like many other institutions in the country, the Djiboutian educational system is based on the French colonial model. But the statistics show that the French educators of the colonial administration did not leave behind a great legacy. At the time of independence in 1977, there were very few high school graduates amongst the native population and only three Djiboutians with university degrees. The new president, who would take over that year and run the country for two decades, only had a sixth-grade education! Today, just 39 percent of Djibouti's school-age population attends primary school, and only 14 percent is enrolled in secondary school.

Djibouti is doing its best to rectify this situation, and strives to ensure that every child receives at least an adequate education. The educational system in Djibouti aims to give all children from about the age of six to the age of eleven a primary school education. From there, students go on to a *lycée*, or secondary school, until age 15, at which point they may have the option of continuing on with their studies. Students choose to go to a university or get a vocational, or trade, education, which is considered less prestigious but offers better employment prospects. Those who opt for a more comprehensive education have few options, however, as Djibouti has no university of its own. Students have to go overseas for their post-secondary schooling, often to France or Morocco, with whom Djibouti signed an educational exchange agreement in 2000.

The People of Djibouti

Population: 472,810

Ethnic groups: Somali 60%, Afar 35%, French, Arab, Ethiopian, and Italian 5%

Religions: Muslim 94%, Christian 6%

Language: French (official), Arabic (official), Somali, Afar

Age structure:
  0–14 years: 42.6%
  15–64 years: 54.5%
  65 years and over: 2.9%

Population growth rate: 2.59%

Birth rate: 40.33 births/1,000 population

Death rate: 14.43/1,000 population

Infant mortality rate: 99.7/1,000 live births

Life expectancy at birth:
  total population: 51.6 years
  males: 49.73 years
  females: 53.52 years

Total fertility rate: 5.64 children born/woman

Literacy: 46.2% (1995 est.)

All figures are 2002 estimates unless otherwise indicated.
Source: Adapted from CIA World Factbook, 2002.

Unfortunately, many factors conspire to keep Djibouti from achieving the educational excellence to which the government aspires. Child labor has long been prevalent in the country, forcing kids to work before they have completed the basic requirements in school. Discrimination against females is also a major problem, for young girls and women in the job market. Because a Djiboutian girl has even less of a chance than a Djiboutian boy to find paid employment as an adult, she is less likely to be educated and more likely to face a life of domestic duty in her family's home—and eventually, the home of her husband's family. The final factor working against Djibouti's educational system is the nomadic lifestyle of many citizens, which make it virtually impossible for many children ever to see the inside of a classroom.

QAT

Commonly used across eastern Africa and Yemen on the Arabian Peninsula, *qat,* or *Catha edulis*, is a plant whose leaves,

Ethiopian smugglers carry sacks of *qat* leaves, a popular stimulant, to the Djibouti border. Eight tons of *qat* arrives daily to Djibouti by plane, and a good portion of the afternoon and evening is devoted to chewing the leaf at home in *mabrazes,* or *qat* dens. The government, concerned about how *qat* hampers productivity, unsuccessfully tried to make the drug illegal in 1977.

Djiboutian women in traditional costume perform a tribal dance. The age-old dances of Djibouti exhibit both Arab and African influences. Many dances celebrate special events and rites of passage; war dances prepare tribesmen for an upcoming battle.

when chewed, produce a mildly stimulating effect. It is like the coca plant of South America, from which cocaine is extracted, though the effect of *qat* on the user is less potent. *Qat*-chewing, also popular in Somalia, Ethiopia, and Yemen, is so common that it is considered a national addiction and is estimated, by some accounts, to be responsible for at least a whopping 40 percent of the average household's budget expenses. Eight tons of *qat* are flown in every day from Ethiopia; when it arrives to Djibouti town, almost always at 1:20 P.M., virtually all of the city's activities come to a halt. Many Djiboutis will then retire to their *mabraz*, or *qat* den, where they will sit around for as long as five hours at a stretch, chewing *qat*, smoking cigarettes, and drinking tea.

Although this may seem like a charming custom to some, and *qat* generates government revenue as a taxed import, the widesread use of the drug hampers the country's economic productivity and social unity. Not only does this leisure activity consume much of the small income of the average Djiboutian, the consumption of *qat* also causes constant domestic strife, largely because of the toll it takes on family budgets. In addition, untold working hours and productivity are chewed away in the habit. Some people even argue that the drug may worsen ethnic tensions—or at the very least keep them from improving—since members of a tribe chew exclusively at their respective *mabrazes* and nowhere else. The practice, some believe, further isolates the Afars and Issas, sustaining the lack of understanding between the two tribes.

The government has attempted on more than one occasion to address the *qat* problem; most notably, the Aptidon regime tried to ban the drug outright in 1977. But as the United States learned during the years between 1920 and 1933, when alcohol was made illegal, it is nearly impossible to keep a populace from getting what so much of it enjoys and wants. Aptidon's attempt to outlaw *qat* met with almost immediate failure: massive protests broke out in absolutely every quarter of society. A *qat* black market also sprung up, and the government was forced to give up its agenda of prohibition. Ironically, the protests managed to briefly bring together members of rival ethnic tribes to fight a common cause.

ARTS AND CULTURE

Despite its poverty and other problems, Djibouti has developed a sophisticated culture that is particularly evident in its handicrafts.

One practical craft that is unique to Djibouti is the weaving of **fiddimas**, or Afar mats. These mats, which women design and weave out of palm-tree leaves, serve a variety of purposes. People use them as prayer rugs, sleeping mattress, or even wraps for the deceased.

Similar to handwoven Persian carpets, a popular commodity of Islamic societies, Afar mats have many different patterns, each of which has a special significance. Among the various designs are those that signify good luck, fertility, and the mat-maker's place of origin. Djiboutians take pride in their mats, and the mat-making craft inspires a lot of good-natured competition among weavers, all striving to make the most beautiful and elaborate *fiddima*. The best mats often make for valuable gifts. Some families demand at least 50 mats for just one bridal dowry.

Henna is a popular form of body makeup in Djibouti. The women pick henna plant leaves and crush them to extract a brown dye. To darken the dye, they mix in lemon juice or kohl, a traditional kind of eye makeup. Women most commonly draw the elaborate henna designs on their hands or feet.

Fashion generally follows Islamic custom in Djibouti. Women cover themselves with long skirts or dresses, over which they wear a *shamma*, a see-through, brightly colored piece of fabric. A traditional garment for men is the *foutah*, a thin strip of cloth that is worn as a long skirt.

The music and dance traditions of the Afars and Issas show both African and Arab influences. Djibouti is known for its traditional tribal dances, accompanied by rhythmic drumming, that mark special events and rites of passage. Dances include the *barimo*, performed at weddings by men and women in pairs; the *hirwo*, a rain dance; and the *barri horra* and the *wiwileh*, war dances designed to gear up those preparing for an upcoming battle.

Besides these traditional dances, Djibouti also boasts a number of modern musicians. Some of the most popular artists manage to combine modern soul and jazz styles with traditional Djiboutian rhythms, and regularly perform concerts across Europe.

A young woman trains on a sewing machine in a Djibouti City classroom. In addition to maintaining the primary industries of shipping and fishing, city leaders focus on textiles and other developing industries.

Communities

Djibouti's harsh climate has not entirely eliminated the nomadic lifestyle of the tribespeople, but it has persuaded many fighting drought and starvation to move to the capital city. Two-thirds of the country's population, which the Central Intelligence Agency (CIA) estimated at 472,810 in 2002, lives in Djibouti town. These numbers make Djibouti the most highly urbanized country on the continent of Africa. Poverty is widespread among city dwellers, as many struggle to adapt their tribal lifestyle to modern city life.

There are four major towns that fall behind the port of Djibouti in population: Obock, Dikhil, Ali Sabieh, and Tadjoura. Dikhil, located in the desert along the border with Ethiopia, had an estimated 87,900 people in 2003, making it Djibouti's second-largest city. Obock and Tadjoura, located on the Gulf of Tadjoura, receive many visitors to the country with their natural attractions and old Arabian architecture.

PORT OF DJIBOUTI

Since it became the capital city of French Somaliland in 1892, Djibouti town has been the object of criticism among many foreigners stopping there on their way to somewhere else, as well as those living there for several years at a colonial posting. American journalist David Lamb described his mixed impression of the capital city just after the country gained its independance. In his account, Djibouti town

> had only two factories, one for bottling Coca-Cola, the other for bottling Pepsi, and almost everything except a few home-grown tomatoes was imported: table salt from Holland, vegetables and eggs from Ethiopia, meat from Kenya, drinking water from France. . . .
>
> Djibouti . . . was a wonderfully seedy place. . . . There was a dingy square, Place Menelik, surrounded by cafés and bars nestled under urine-drenched arches. French soldiers and civilians sat at the tables there, shirts unbuttoned to the waist, sweating in the 100-degree evening heat, swilling lukewarm beer and chasing away the swarming beggars with a wave of a hand. At night the foreigners retreated behind louvered shutters in shabby villas on streets like the Rue de Beauchamps and Avenue Pasteur. The Africans lived on the other side of town, in shacks made of packing crates. . . .
>
> The atmosphere of Djibouti was reminiscent of Saigon circa 1950. The elegance was gone, but a faded charm lingered. Everything needed painting and sweeping. The sun beat down like a hammer, and everyone moved slowly, concerned with little except the arrival of siesta time, which stretched from eleven-thirty to four.

Beyond the echoes of its colonial past, Djibouti does not have the prominence and rich history of most capital cities. It is hard to ignore the fact that the city's original inception over a century ago was for the convenience of the ruling colonial power. There is very little in the way of former imperial grandeur, such as the once-grand palaces of other colonial capitals that have since been converted to museums. Djibouti town is laid out in a series of

Leopard skins are displayed at a market stand in Djibouti City, Djibouti. Industry is limited in the country—in 2003, the capital city only had two main factories. City merchants and businesses generally rely on imports for their sources of revenue.

zones, or quarters, among them the Place Menelik, the city's business district; the Plateau du Serpent, the wealthy district dominated by rich foreign residents; and the Place Rimbaud, home to a majority of the natives.

Also, unlike many capitals of the old French empire, Djibouti town's architecture is more Arab than French. The building materials, cut coral blocks and cement also made from coral, are completely indigenous to the region. Most buildings are square, two-story affairs, often with terraces running the entire perimeter of the structures. To keep the buildings and houses of Djibouti town naturally cool in the sweltering summer heat, people have built thick walls and have whitewashed them to better reflect the sun's hot rays. Perforated window screens, many with intricate designs, help to keep the air circulating in the home.

Shipping and fishing are the city's main economic activities. Because many of the city's Issas are devout Muslims, they enjoy a fair amount of success as traders and intermediaries with the Arab merchants from across the Bab el Mandeb. Those able to get away from their shipping and fishing duties can enjoy Djibouti town's beaches, which most agree are the city's most picturesque spots. The surrounding water offers some of the most startlingly beautiful marine life on the planet.

A faded plaque in Obock proclaims Comte (Count) Leonce Lagarde as the "founder of Djibouti." The French first settled French Somaliland at Obock in 1862; thirty years later, they moved the capital to the port of Djibouti, which offered better access to the Bab el Mandeb Strait.

OTHER CITIES AND TOWNS

Although Djibouti town is the country's biggest attraction and holds the largest segment of the population, other communities still have their merits. Obock, the first administrative capital of the French territory, presents a fascinating glimpse of modern Djiboutian history. Located across the Gulf of Tadjoura from Djibouti town, Obock became a bustling town of 2,000 people just six years after the French bought what we now call Djibouti from the local sultans.

Today Obock is a shadow of its former self, though the town is still home to a great deal of historic architecture, which some say is more impressive than the architecture of Djibouti town. And, in a limited way, Obock is opening itself up to the tourist trade as the jumping-off point for scuba diving tours. Divers come from all over the world to see the spectacular marine life of the Red Sea coral reefs.

Directly across the Tadjoura Gulf lies a settlement named after the gulf. Tadjoura is striking for a variety of reasons, not the least of which is that it has traditionally been an Arabian center in Djibouti. The Arabian sultans who sold what was then the Territory of Afars and Issas to the French had their headquarters there. It is also one of the oldest surviving towns or trading posts on the East African coast, and there are references to it in Arabian literature as far back as the 12th century. Today the town is largely an Afar community, and it manufactures the beautiful, long daggers called *poignards* that are carried by all Afar tribesmen. Nonetheless, the town's architecture reflects the country's Arabian heritage, perhaps more than any place else in Djibouti.

Lying approximately 75 miles (120 km) southwest of Djibouti City is Dikhil, which is an important town for a number of reasons. The French set up an administrative post here in 1928, and today

An Ethiopian man washes a young child in a refugee camp outside Djibouti City. Most of the country's refugees come from Ethiopia and Somalia, and the camps are administered by international agencies such as the United Nations, which runs this one.

it remains a regional capital. Also, it has been a meeting and market center for the local nomadic tribes throughout history. Perched on a rocky ledge and surrounded by an ancient palm grove, it is still a thriving population center. In 2003, some 35,000 people lived in Dikhil, despite the greater employment opportunities that Djibouti town offers.

REFUGEE CAMPS

Typically, refugee camps are not major population centers, but Djibouti is an exception: at times there have been as many as 200,000 refugees in the country, mostly from Ethiopia and Somalia. Generally located in remote areas far from Djibouti town, the refugee zones often place members of rival tribes in close proximity. Not surprisingly, these zones are where most of Djibouti's regional conflicts have developed.

The camps are administered by a variety of international bodies and non-governmental organizations, including the United Nations. Predictably, refugees living in these camps are completely dependent on foreign and external sources of food and water since they are in the middle of the Djiboutian desert, where raising animals or farming is not an option. For the most part, Djibouti has done its best to keep the refugee population from becoming a permanent fixture in their country; the government has successfully repatriated, or sent home to a more stable situation, hundreds of thousands of refugees since the first group of refugees sought asylum in 1988.

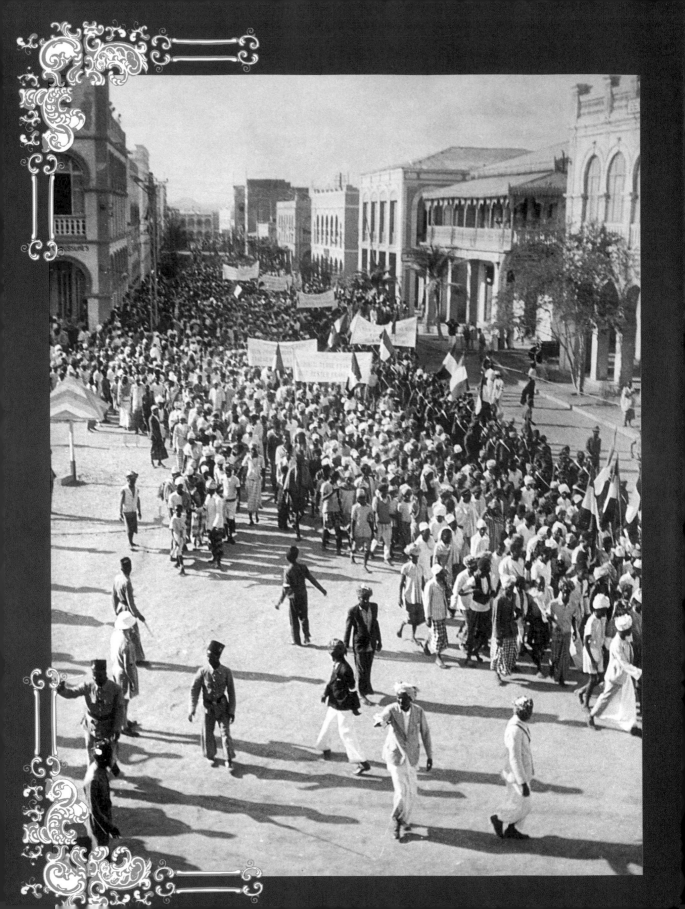

Hundreds of Djiboutians march through the capital city's streets in 1939, protesting Italy's territorial demands on what was then French Somaliland. Throughout its history as an independant republic, Djibouti has had improved relations with Western countries, especially with the United States and France.

Foreign Relations

Djibouti is a small country living in one of the world's roughest neighborhoods. If it did not devote a great deal of time and energy toward foreign affairs, the tiny country could very well get sucked into the turbulence around it. Surrounded by—and ethnically linked to—countries that have been broken up by civil wars (Eritrea and Ethiopia) and those have seen internal disputes spill over their own borders (Somalia), Djibouti has still managed to navigate the waters of international conflict with modest success, finding assistance from the United Nations and regional agencies devoted to establishing and maintaining peace. Djibouti has also adroitly handled its diplomatic relations with the West, and has avoided demonstrating the anti-American and anti-European attitude that has caused many of its neighbors to become isolated.

Since Djibouti became an independent nation, the French have set up "listening posts," highly classified intelligence operations that many believe allow Paris to listen in on radio and telephone communications throughout the Middle East.

RELATIONS WITH THE WEST

Since achieving independence in 1977, Djibouti has sought to maintain good relations with the Western powers, including the United States and France, the country's former colonial overlord. Its approach has been somewhat of a surprise, given that after gaining their independence, many former colonies have striven to cut off diplomatic and economic ties with their mother countries to prove that they can make their own way. Perhaps the leaders of Djibouti acknowledged that with the country's trying financial circumstances, taking an independent path would involve taking some major economic risks.

For years, the government had welcomed a garrison of French troops numbering around 4,000, which eventually declined to 2,600. Their presence has been a major help in fending off the advances of ambitious neighbors. Describing the small country's situation after gaining its independence, a French naval officer told a British photojournalist: "Djibouti is as helpless as a goat that two lions are waiting to pounce on. We guard the goat."

Of course, the French do not just guard Djibouti for the sheer pleasure of protecting a former colony. Their stake in Djibouti allows them to control, should they ever need or want to, the strategically critical Bab el Mandeb, which connects the Red Sea to the Indian Ocean. The French military also operates several permanent bases in Djibouti.

Since the United States and Djibouti established diplomatic ties in 1977, Djibouti has continually relied on American aid through the US Agency for International Development (USAID). In 2000, the United States provided approximately $7 million in aid to Djibouti for various programs. Djibouti is one of few Muslim countries that have a strong relationship with the United States, and has a long history of supporting U.S. policy in the Middle East. During the Persian Gulf War, Djibouti was highly supportive of the American effort to oust the Iraqi army from Kuwait, which it had recently invaded. It offered itself as a base for French troops, who fought with the alliance against Saddam Hussein. It also became a place to regroup for the armies from several coalition countries, including the United States.

Djibouti has continued to support the United States in the 21st

President Ismael Omar Guelleh announced in December 2002 that Djibouti would remain committed to helping Western coalition forces in the "war on terrorism." The U.S. and French militaries have bases in Djibouti, from which intelligence has been gathered about possible terrorist activity in the Horn of Africa. Djibouti's government hopes to receive international aid in exchange for its cooperation with the West.

century. After the terrorist attacks of September 11, 2001, the government expressed its deep regret and sympathy to the U.S. Once again, Djibouti came through by providing assistance to the Western forces searching for the al-Qaeda masterminds behind the attacks. Since August 2002, the country has allowed 800 American soldiers to be stationed at Djibouti town's Le Monier barracks, and another contingent set up operations at Obock across the Gulf of Tadjoura. Germany also had more than 1,200 soldiers stationed in Djibouti. The U.S. and German militaries used Djibouti as a base of operations to try to track down al-Qaeda members, who have been reported to have training camps in the Horn of Africa as well as in regions of the Middle East. The United States believed that those fleeing Afghanistan, where their camps were bombarded by U.S. forces in late 2001, were possibly headed to the Horn of Africa to find refuge. Some even suspected that the al-Qaeda leader, Osama bin Laden, might use this region as an escape route. In March 2003, a second war in Iraq broke out. American forces stationed in Djibouti prepared for possible deployment to the Persian Gulf.

The people of Djibouti were generally positive about the presence of American troops on their soil. When asked about the prospect of more U.S. soldiers coming to town, one local Djiboutian told reporters, "For us, it's good because we can make conversation with them and maybe have some jobs when more of them come. We like to have Americans here." The U.S. bases only could offer a limited number of jobs, however, which meant many Djiboutians looking for work were disappointed. In return for allowing troops to be stationed and trained on its soil, the United States made initial plans to reopen the Djibouti town office of the Agency for International Development, which in the mid-1990s had been shut down due to a lack of funding.

Despite its friendly gestures toward Western nations, including its cooperation with the United States in the "war on terrorism," Djibouti has always refused to recognize Israel as an official country. Like its Arab neighbors across the Bab el Mandeb strait, Djibouti has never had relations with the Jewish state, asserting that Israel occupies land rightfully belonging to the Arabs of the region.

AFRICAN NEIGHBORS OF THE HORN

Djibouti's relations with neighboring countries have always been a tricky affair. Since achieving independence, Djibouti has sought

A peaceful street message greets pedestrians in Arta, Djibouti, where leaders of the Horn of Africa assembled in 2000 to reconcile warring factions in Somalia and establish a provisional government. Djibouti has remained involved in healing war-torn Somalia through organizations like the Intergovernmental Authority for Development (IGAD) in Eastern Africa, whose headquarters is located in Djibouti.

to remain neutral even as its neighbors have waged war for decades, but the government has been hard-pressed to reconcile rival peoples while preserving its neutral role. During the 1980s, what further complicated the issue for Djibouti was the influence of the Cold War on the region's disputes. The Cold War was a shifting power struggle between the Western powers, led by the United States, and the Communist bloc, led by the former Soviet Union. Each power was seeking for ways to edge the other's influence out of regions across the globe, including the Horn of Africa.

Ethiopian soldiers march toward Tigray, just south of the Eritrean border, during the border war between the two countries (1998–2000). Djibouti managed to take some of Eritrea's trade during the conflict, though the country also suffered another wave of war refugees.

Neutrality has become less feasible as Djibouti struggles to live in the dangerous environment of the Horn of Africa. Nonetheless, since 1986 Djibouti has worked actively to decrease tension in the region and promote stability, working with the East African organization IGAD (Intergovernmental Authority on Development) to bring warring parties together. Through its mediating role, Djibouti has earned from its African neighbors such nicknames as "the eye of the storm" and "a neutral gatehouse on the Red Sea."

The Ogaden War of 1977–78 was the first major test of Djibouti's diplomatic capabilities. Shortly after the country became an official state, this war broke out between its neighbors Ethiopia and Somalia. The conflict had been brewing for ages; the Ogaden region of southeastern Ethiopia, near the Somalian border, has long been an Islamic stronghold (in contrast with the rest of the country, which is predominantly Christian). Eventually, fighting broke out as a Somali guerrilla group, supported by the aid and quiet approval of the Somali government, began a series of cross-border raids into Ethiopia. And suddenly, the Ethiopians found themselves on the losing end of a war they did not want and—so it seemed at the time—could not win.

Ethiopia had little chance of keeping the Ogaden until it decided to appeal to the Soviet Union for help. Although the Soviets had traditionally backed Somalia, they saw Ethiopians as a more suitable ally and switched sides. With the Soviet's valuable support, the Ethiopians mounted a devastating assault on the Ogaden. The Ethiopian victories produced the large numbers of refugees who soon entered Djibouti. The end of the war came quickly, and by early 1978, with the help of Soviet equipment and Cuban troops, the Ethiopians had driven the Somalis back to the border. On an entirely separate front, Ethiopia and its allies were able to crush Eritrean nationalists and reclaim land Eritreans had won two years earlier.

Djibouti had great difficulties coping with the war so soon after its independence. Waves of refugees streamed into the country, though Djibouti could ill afford to take care of them. Even worse, during the war the railway from Addis Ababa to Djibouti was temporarily cut off, destroying trade and shutting down most of the port's activity. In short, the Ogaden War was an unmitigated disaster from which Djibouti took years to recover.

Many years later, in 1998, another war broke out in the region that was to have profound consequences for Djibouti's relations with neighboring states. A border conflict between Ethiopia and Eritrea, which had won its independence from its larger neighbor five years earlier, broke out over territory that the new state considered rightfully its own. Over the next two and a half years, at least 70,000 were killed, land mines rendered huge swaths of territory inhospitable, and untold thousands of people were made refugees, swelling Djibouti's foreign population even further.

However, Djibouti was able to find one material benefit of this war. During the fighting, Ethiopia lost its access to the Red Sea along Eritrea's coast, and so had to turn exclusively to Djibouti's trade avenues. As a result, the port of Djibouti and the Addis Ababa–Djibouti railroad thrived. In 1998 alone, port traffic tripled, and the country started to experience an upturn in business and employment prospects. On the downside, Djibouti's close dealings with Ethiopia had soured its relations with both Somalia and Eritrea.

Djibouti has done all possible to repair relations as well reclaim its role as peacemaker of the region. The government has called for a return to a civil society in Somalia, which in recent years has broken down into a bloody civil war fought by rampaging warlords. Djibouti has been pivotal in setting up conferences aimed at establishing some semblance of order in Somalia. At the first meeting, the Djibouti-sponsored Arta Peace Conference in 2000, Abdulkassim Salat Hassan was voted the interim president of

Somalia's newly formed Transitional National Government. The Intergovernmental Authority for Development (IGAD) in Eastern Africa, made up of seven member states, has also worked toward reconciling Somalia's warring factions. Along with promoting peace and stability, the organization, headquartered in Djibouti, also aims to find multilateral solutions to the resource shortages so common in this part of the world.

ca. 3,200,000 B.C.: "Lucy," one of the oldest known human-like creatures, is believed to have lived in the Afar Triangle near Djibouti.

ca. 1,500,000 B.C.: Ancestors of modern man settle around Lac Abbe in today's Djibouti.

4000 B.C.: Settlers in Djibouti construct giant basalt millstones and obsidian tools.

2nd century B.C.: The kingdom of Aksum develops in modern-day Ethiopia.

1st century B.C.: The kingdom of Aksum grows to incorporate what today is called Djibouti.

4th century A.D.: Christianity is established in the kingdom of Aksum.

570: Muhammad is born in Mecca on the Arabian Peninsula.

ca. 700: Aksum begins 300-year decline; Islam begins to spread along the African coast.

975: Muslim warriors advance on kingdom of Aksum, but fail to convert the region of Djibouti.

1542: After nearly three centuries of resisting Islam, Djibouti and other small states of the Horn of Africa finally convert.

1862: France purchases Djibouti from local Ottoman sultans; French Somaliland is born.

1869: The Suez Canal is opened, vastly increasing the strategic importance of French Somaliland.

1892: The French move the colonial capital to Djibouti town.

1897: Work begins on the Addis Ababa–Djibouti railroad.

1917: The Addis Ababa–Djibouti railroad is completed.

1957: French Somaliland is re-organized as the Territory of Afars and Issas, with much greater freedom to run its own affairs.

1967: An independence referendum fails by a margin of 60 percent to 40 percent; the Six-Day War closes down Suez Canal, which in turn injures Djibouti's economy.

1977: After an independence referendum passes, the modern Republic of Djibouti is born on June 27; war breaks out between Ethiopia and Somalia over the Ogaden region.

CHRONOLOGY

1978: The Ogaden War ends; Djibouti struggles to handle thousands of refugees caused by the fighting.

1981: Opposition parties are banned; incumbent President Aptidon wins a six-year term of office.

1987: Aptidon is once again re-elected to another six-year term of office.

1991: Fierce fighting breaks out between Afar rebels and the Aptidon government.

1994: Peace agreement is signed between Afar rebels and the government; leaders of the insurgency are allowed positions in the new government.

1998: War breaks out between Ethiopia and Eritrea; 70,000 people are killed and hundreds of thousands of refugees stream into Djibouti.

1999: Aptidon steps down and is replaced in an election by his nephew and chief of staff, Ismael Omar Guelleh.

2000: In August, Djibouti hosts the Somali National Peace Conference in Arta.

2002: President Guelleh negotiates deal with United States to station troops fighting the "war on terrorism" in Djibouti; in August, U.S. troops arrive in search of any al-Qaeda members that might be hiding in the Horn of Africa.

2003: In January, a coalition led by Guelleh wins Djibouti's multi-party elections. In March, a second war breaks out in Iraq and U.S. troops in Djibouti await possible deployment to the Persian Gulf.

Afar Triangle—part of the Great Rift Valley, a geologic depression in the Horn of Africa that contains Djibouti as well as Eritrea and part of Ethiopia.

Afars—the minority tribal group in Djibouti; many are nomads with ancestral ties to Ethiopian tribes.

Aksum—a huge empire that encompassed Djibouti and much of the Horn of Africa for centuries before the coming of Islam.

fiddimas—also known as Afar mats; small, colorful mattresses intricately woven out of palm leaves.

Great Rift Valley—a massive geological split in the continent of Africa running through the eastern part of the continent from Egypt to South Africa.

hajj—the pilgrimage to Mecca, which every capable male Muslim is required to make at least once in his life.

Horn of Africa—the geographic reference to the area containing Djibouti, Ethiopia, Eritrea, and Somalia.

Issas—the main Somali tribal group in Djibouti; traditionally nomadic and fervent Muslims, they have had power over the Afars throughout much of Djibouti's history.

Ka'aba—the sacred stone in Mecca; Muslims face in its direction during daily prayers.

lycée—a French-style secondary school that every Djiboutian is supposed to attend.

Mecca—the hometown of the prophet Muhammad, from which he eventually fled persecution.

Medina—the city where Islam was founded; next to Mecca, the holiest city of Islam.

Monophysite—meaning "one form" or "one nature," the term applied to those who believe in the total and complete divinity of Jesus Christ.

obsidian—a dark glass formed by the cooling of molten lava.

polytheistic—believing in more than one god.

Qur'an—the Muslim holy book; dictated by the prophet Muhammad in the seventh century A.D.

Ramadan—the month of the Islamic calendar during which Muslims fast from sunrise to sunset.

GLOSSARY

rer—a large congregation of families; the fundamental social unit of the Issas.

Shahada—the central prayer and basic statement of belief of all Muslims.

Sharia—a civil legal code based on the Qur'an that supplements the Djiboutian legal system.

tectonic plates—the large geological pieces of the earth's crust on which the continents sit.

topographical—having a map design based on the natural features of the earth.

xeer—traditional tribal law that is often used to settle civil disputes in Djibouti.

FURTHER READING

Caputo, Philip. *Horn of Africa.* New York: Vintage Books, 2002.

Celati, Gianni. *Adventures in Africa*, trans. Adria Berhardi. Chicago: Chicago University Press, 2000.

Connah, Graham. *African Civilizations: Precolonial Cities and States in Tropical Africa.* Cambridge, England: Cambridge University Press, 1987.

Finlay, Hugh. *Africa on a Shoestring.* Melbourne: Lonely Planet Publications, 2001.

Grove, A. T. *The Changing Geography of Africa.* Oxford, England: Oxford University Press, 1994.

Hamaleinen, Pertti, and Frances Linzee Gordon. *Lonely Planet Guide to Ethiopia, Eritrea and Djibouti.* Melbourne: Lonely Planet Publications, 1999.

Kaplan, Marion. *Focus Africa: A Photojournalist's Perspective.* London: Elm Tree Books, 1983.

Lamb, David. *The Africans.* New York: Vintage Books, 1987.

Toggia, Pietro, Lauderdale, Pat, and Abebe Zegeye, eds. *Crisis and Terror in the Horn of Africa.* Kent: Ashgate Publishing Limited, 2000.

INTERNET RESOURCES

Djibouti has almost no Internet access; so not surprisingly, there are few Internet resources about this tiny land, and very few in English. The following are the most useful sites:

http://www.arab.net/djibouti/index.html

This site offers a basic overview of Djibouti, as well as general information about the Arab world.

http://www.cia.gov/cia/publications/factbook/geos/dj.html

An up-to-date fact sheet on Djibouti provided by the CIA. Includes map of the country.

http://allafrica.com/djibouti/

A useful resource for information on current events in Djibouti. Includes links to more general sites covering eastern Africa and the rest of the continent.

http://www.lonelyplanet.com/destinations/africa/djibouti/

An informative tourist site published by Lonely Planet Guides. Features write-ups of Djibouti's most popular tourist attractions.

Numbers in **bold italic** refer to captions.

INDEX

PICTURE CREDITS

CONTRIBUTORS

The **FOREIGN POLICY RESEARCH INSTITUTE (FPRI)** served as editorial consultants for the MODERN MIDDLE EAST NATIONS series. FPRI is one of the nation's oldest "think tanks." The Institute's Middle East Program focuses on Gulf security, monitors the Arab-Israeli peace process, and sponsors an annual conference for teachers on the Middle East, plus periodic briefings on key developments in the region.

Among the FPRI's trustees is a former Secretary of State and a former Secretary of the Navy (and among the FPRI's former trustees and interns, two current Undersecretaries of Defense), not to mention two university presidents emeritus, a foundation president, and several active or retired corporate CEOs.

The scholars of FPRI include a former aide to three U.S. Secretaries of State, a Pulitzer Prize–winning historian, a former president of Swarthmore College and a Bancroft Prize–winning historian, and two former staff members of the National Security Council. And the FPRI counts among its extended network of scholars—especially its Inter-University Study Groups—representatives of diverse disciplines, including political science, history, economics, law, management, religion, sociology, and psychology.

DR. HARVEY SICHERMAN is president and director of the Foreign Policy Research Institute in Philadelphia, Pennsylvania. He has extensive experience in writing, research, and analysis of U.S. foreign and national security policy, both in government and out. He served as Special Assistant to Secretary of State Alexander M. Haig Jr. and as a member of the Policy Planning Staff of Secretary of State James A. Baker III. Dr. Sicherman was also a consultant to Secretary of the Navy John F. Lehman Jr. (1982–1987) and Secretary of State George Shultz (1988).

A graduate of the University of Scranton (B.S., History, 1966), Dr. Sicherman earned his Ph.D. at the University of Pennsylvania (Political Science, 1971), where he received a Salvatori Fellowship. He is author or editor of numerous books and articles, including *America the Vulnerable: Our Military Problems and How to Fix Them* (FPRI, 2002) and *Palestinian Autonomy, Self-Government and Peace* (Westview Press, 1993). He edits *Peacefacts*, an FPRI bulletin that monitors the Arab-Israeli peace process.

From his first trips to Egypt and Kenya as a high school student, **JAMES MORROW** has been fascinated by the Middle East and Africa. In the years since, he has had numerous opportunities to study and write about the region, first as a student at Georgetown University's School of Foreign Service and later as a journalist for a wide range of publications, including *U.S. News & World Report*, *National Review*, and *The Australian* newspaper. He currently divides his time between Sydney, Australia, and New York City, with his wife Claire (without her research assistance this book would not have been possible), and their son Nicholas.